United All-Time Greats

Greats

Heroes of the Stretford End

United All-Time Greats

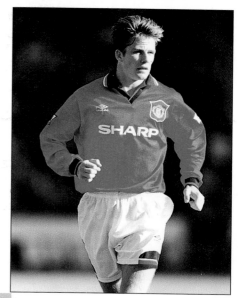

Heroes of the Stretford End

S

SIENA

Above: Kevin Moran beats Norwich keeper
Chris Woods to score for United, 1985.

Siena
PO Box 14840
London NW3 5WT

ISBN 0-75252-376-7

Contents

Introduction

Manchester is a very special city, and Manchester United is a very special team. That much is clear to anybody with even a passing interest in the game of football. And when the United team, fresh from their fourth Premiership crown in five years, were presented to the Prince of Wales in a show to mark the 21st anniversary of the Prince's

Trust in 1997, they were acclaimed with as much fervour as pop sensations the Spice Girls, who were nominally top of the bill.

This was no accident, for United's side of 1996-97 had as much teen appeal as any sporting outfit the world over. Ryan Giggs combined wing skills with the dark good looks that made him a pin-up on the bedroom walls of both sexes, while Eric Cantona's

Right: Unlike his friend George Graham, with whom he shares this photo opportunity, United manager Alex Ferguson (left) has rarely let go of the FA Carling Premiership trophy. The Red Devils have claimed the title four times out of a possible five since its inauguration.

enigmatic appeal saw his shock retirement make as many column inches in the broadsheets as the tabloids. England man David Beckham, 22, was rumoured to be the romantic target of several pop starlets (including, whisper it quietly, a Spice Girl), while the rest of the team, from blond Norse god Peter Schmeichel in goal to Cole and Solskjaer up front, combined skill to wow the boys with looks to thrill the ladies.

ICONS

Little wonder that the team of 1996-97 were idols to all ages and sexes – and it was no surprise, either, to find Old Trafford over-subscribed, as fans sought to view their idols at the closest of close quarters. Yet, United followers of a certain age could look back to the club's last period of sustained success under Matt Busby and point to the 'Babes' who had a similar appeal, before the tragic air crash at Munich in 1958 tore the team apart. And then there was the side of 1968 which, by winning the European Cup, set Alex Ferguson's team the ultimate target.

Until the biggest prize in European club football was back in the Old Trafford trophy room, the jury would still be out as to where the current side stood in relation to their predecessors. Peter Schmeichel went public with his belief that the team of 1996-97 would beat the past masters – decisively! But though a TV advertisement successfully deceived the eye by blending film footage of stars of old and new, the art of comparison is at best an imprecise one. And even if 'Fergie's Fledglings' become Champions of Europe, names like Charlton, Best, Crerand and Law will never be erased from football's – and United's – roll of honour.

KINGS OF ROCK'N'ROLL

Whether or not you subscribe to the view that football is the 'new rock'n'roll', it is indisputable that Manchester United are the game's biggest names. What this book hopes to do is to put the stars of the current team in context with some of the greats that preceded them onto the pitch at Old Trafford. The hallowed turf there is the stage of the

'Theatre of Dreams': little wonder that Giggs, Cantona and company showed little stage-fright when they took their royal bow.

Like Coronation Street, that timeless television soap opera that's entranced the nation for nearly four decades, the name and reputation of Manchester United is part of the nation's consciousness. Sky Television enables the millions who can't get tickets to partake of the experience, making them as familiar a sight as politicians and pop stars. Which is where we came in. If, like the Spice Girls, you 'Wannabe' well informed, then turn the pages here as United stars of past and present are profiled in words and colour pictures.

Above: Denis Irwin, a stalwart performer and Eire international adding experience to Alex Ferguson's late-1990s Fledglings.

7

Manchester United Club History

I n a football world where national barriers are rapidly becoming meaningless, the name of Manchester United has always been a watchword. The first English club to compete in Europe, they garnered the sympathy of a nation after the Munich air crash that decimated their team in 1958, coming back in the 1960s to win first Championships and then the ultimate prize – the European Cup.

Along the way, they picked up some players who would become household names. These included star Scottish striker Denis Law, the first £100,000 player in British football; Bobby Charlton, a Munich survivor and 1966 World Cup winner; George Best, the gifted but wayward Irishman whose skills were unforgettable; and now the international cocktail of Ryan Giggs (Wales), Ole Gunnar Solskjaer (Norway) and recently retired Frenchman, Eric Cantona.

In 1993, the name of Manchester United was first to be inscribed on the new FA Carling Premiership trophy. It's been the only name so far, apart from Blackburn's single-season success of 1994-95 – and twice in the 1990s United have achieved the Double – the Championship and FA Cup in the same season. That's history in the making.

Blasts from United's past: the FA Cup winners of 1909, who beat Bristol City by a single goal (above); George Vose, a local-born defender who helped the club back to the top flight in 1935-36 (right); and John Hanlon, another star of the inter-war period (far right).

Opposite: Legendary manager Sir Matt Busby.

A FOOTBALL ALLIANCE

Their 120-year story started in 1878 when a group of railwaymen formed Newton Heath football team. Playing in the Football Alliance, they obtained Football League status in 1892. The Heathens had endured a chequered history, when in 1902 they were re-financed by a local brewer and renamed Manchester United. Within six years, the Red Devils had claimed their first League Championship, and under the leadership of Welshman Billy Meredith, signed from neighbours City, would secure the FA Cup in 1909 and a second title win in 1911.

But if supporters celebrating their move into a new ground thought the stage was set for decades of hope and glory, they were mistaken. Old Trafford, that legendary latter-day Theatre of Dreams, would remain trophy-free for nearly four decades as rivals City scooped the honours. Ironically, it would be one of their players, Matt Busby, who, after World War II, would change his colours to lead United into a brave new era.

The rivalry with City would become one of the fiercest in football, and kicked off in earnest with an FA Cup tie in 1891. At that point, City were still known as Ardwick – but it was more a case of 'ard luck as they slumped to a 5-1 defeat in front of a 10,000 crowd. Newton Heath

(United) won the first League encounter too by five goals to two, and when the all-time record was calculated as City slid to the Football League in 1996, it stood at 49-32 in United's favour, with 44 draws.

Old Trafford was the target of German bombers during wartime, and rivalry with City was forgotten as United accepted their neighbours' offer and moved into Maine Road while the necessary repairs were carried out.

The FA Cup in 1948 was a bright start for Busby and United, while three League titles were added in the 1950s with what was a young and promising side. Not for nothing were they known as Busby's Babes, and the side he assembled is still considered one of the greatest in English football by those fortunate enough to have seen it.

The likes of Duncan Edwards, captain Roger Byrne and latterly Bobby Charlton were England regulars with at least a decade of top-class football to come. Yet the lives of eight of those stars were claimed by the Munich air crash of February 1958, the careers of several others being cruelly cut short. Manager Matt Busby was given the last rites, but recovered against all odds to build anew.

When United had returned to League football against Sheffield Wednesday, the team formation in the programme had contained 11 blanks. By the early 1960s,

Below: Midfield maestro Pat Crerand was a star of Matt Busby's European Cup-winning side of 1968.

those had disappeared, to be replaced by names like Harry Gregg (a Munich survivor and, at £23,500, the country's most expensive goalkeeper), Denis Law (repatriated from Torino, and, to add spice, a former City star) and Celtic midfielder Pat Crerand, a snip at just £55,000. David Herd and Maurice Setters were less high-profile but equally important signings.

The first trophy to be won was the FA Cup in 1963, the third in United's history. Five years previously, the post-Munich side had reached Wembley on a wave of public emotion, only to lose out controversially to Bolton when Lofthouse bundled Gregg into the net for the second and decisive goal.

This time round, it was United that went 2-0 ahead against Leicester City, and even when the Foxes struck back, the Reds coolly restored their two-goal advantage through Herd to run out easy 3-1 winners. The run to Wembley had taken just eight weeks, this being the season of the 'big freeze' that postponed the Third Round until March.

BUSBY'S GREATEST HOUR
Having waited eight years to take their sixth League title, United bestrode the 1960s like the football colossus they were, by heading the table in both 1965 and 1967.

The first was secured only by goal average over Leeds, who also lost out that year in the Cup to Liverpool. But the win of 1966-67 was achieved in style, having alternated at the top with Liverpool before sealing matters in the penultimate game, with a 6-1 away win at West Ham's Upton Park: 'my greatest hour,' Busby would tell reporters. Denis Law, fed by young winger John Aston, notched 23 League goals that season including two in that game.

The 1965 title had given them a ticket to Europe, but they'd been edged out at the semi-final stage for the third time in their history, bowing to Partizan Belgrade. This time they were in a mood to make it count.

Sure enough, ten years after Munich, United beat Portuguese giants Benfica by four goals to one at Wembley to take the European Cup back to Manchester.

Above: The unique sight of Denis Law thundering in a right-foot special against Crystal Palace.

11

Brian Kidd, the current assistant manager, had been a star in the European Cup Final, deputising for the injured Denis Law, but had it not been for fearless goalkeeping by Alex Stepney, keeping the scores level and forcing extra time, it could have been Eusebio and his team-mates clutching the prize. Two saves in one-on-one situations were absolutely breathtaking – no wonder the Portuguese crumbled.

That historic win sealed United's reputation as the greatest club side in the world – a title the subsequent World Club Championship defeat by Estudiantes of Argentina, a two-legged tie marred by violence and disorder, couldn't erase.

The 1960s had indeed been golden years, and with Matt Busby – now Sir Matt – handing over the reins to ex-player Wilf McGuinness, it seemed a tall order for anyone to replicate a decade of constant success. Bobby Charlton retired in 1973, while George Best let off-field matters destroy his game. He signed off in January 1974

and, though he'd make sporadic comebacks with the likes of Hibernian, Fulham and non-League Dunstable, it was a sad loss to Manchester United and football.

Ex-Leicester boss Frank O'Farrell gave way in late 1972 to much-travelled Scot Tommy Docherty, who gave up the national team to take up the biggest job in football. But neither man, nor their later successors Dave Sexton

Right: The one and only George Best, a talent lost all too soon to the game.

Above right: By contrast, Bobby Charlton has always played the United way as both player and now as club director.

(1977-81) and Ron Atkinson (1981-86), could bring success that was anything better than fleeting. Fifteen years after Busby's swansong, the question posed by Geoffrey Green of The Times, 'Who Can Follow A Living Legend?', would be no nearer being answered.

Under Docherty, United slipped out of the top division for the first time since 1938, their fate cruelly sealed by a goal from former star Denis Law, who'd crossed Manchester for a farewell season with City. And though United came straight back up, fuelled by the goals of Macari and Pearson, Liverpool and Leeds were now mightier forces in League terms.

Ironically, too, local rivals Manchester City had recently enjoyed their most successful period ever under the management duo of Malcolm Allison and Joe Mercer. Though United were victims of a giant-killing in 1976 when losing to Southampton in the FA Cup Final, they beat significantly tougher opposition in Liverpool a year

later. Stuart Pearson and Jimmy Greenhoff destroyed the Merseysiders' hopes of a Treble – League, FA Cup and European Cup – while Arthur Albiston became one of the rare players to make their FA Cup debut in the Final itself when he substituted for Stewart Houston.

Though Cup success was not to be sneezed at, runners-up in 1980 was the closest United would get to the major prize – the League Championship, and with it a passport back to the European Cup. Dave Sexton, one of the game's nice guys and still a respected coach today, made way in 1981 for the extrovert Ron Atkinson. A man whose love of precious metal – at least on the evidence of his penchant for jewellery – would surely bring the serious silverware back to the Old Trafford trophy room.

He did, up to a point – but though United would win the Cup again in 1983 and 1985, the League remained tantalisingly out of reach, despite the arrival of international-class players like Frank Stapleton (Republic

Above left: Ron Atkinson was one of United's more charismatic managers, but unlike his taciturn replacement Alex Ferguson, he could not amass silverware – of the non-wearable variety – in sufficient quantities for the Old Trafford directors.

13

Above: Full-back Lee Martin scores the only goal of the 1990 FA Cup Final win against Crystal Palace – Alex Ferguson's first 'pot' to put in the Old Trafford trophy cabinet.

Right: Tommy Docherty was one of the many managers to ply their trade between the reigns of Busby and Ferguson. None, however, would find lasting success.

of Ireland) and, later, Gordon Strachan (Scotland), together with home-grown teenager Mark Hughes (Wales). Though the consistency wasn't there for a sustained title challenge, there was no doubt that when all these players gelled, United were as attractive as any team in the land.

Englishmen Peter Beardsley and Bryan Robson also arrived, and while the diminutive Tynesider was let go after playing just once, Robson – signed from Atkinson's former club West Bromwich in a £2 million package deal with Remi Moses – would give sterling service over 13 seasons and earn the nickname Captain Marvel for his all-action style.

THE ROAD TO VICTORY

Alongside the captain of industry in midfield, Arnold Muhren became the first Dutchman to play for United when he signed from Ipswich Town in 1982. He'd been Player of the Year at Portman Road in his first season and inspired them to second in the League but, sadly, injury would mean Old Trafford never saw the best of him.

He did however star in the 1983 FA Cup win, a 4-0 replay win against Brighton, the biggest margin in the Final's Wembley history. He scored the fourth goal to help hammer home United's first trophy in six years. European glory in the Cup Winners' Cup seemed more than a possibility the following season, when Barcelona and Diego Maradona were beaten in the quarter-final. Perhaps the effort was too much, for Juventus closed the door in the semis. Heysel was only a season away, and the ban on English teams that followed would keep United's continental ambitions on ice until the 1990s.

The road to the 1985 Cup Final started at Bournemouth where United had bowed out the previous campaign. That hurdle overcome, they faced top-class opposition in the likes of Coventry, West Ham and Liverpool, the latter beaten only after two eventful games, before facing the Merseysiders' closest rivals at Wembley.

This match too was full of incident, and will be remembered for referee Peter Willis's decision to make Kevin Moran the first man ever to be dismissed in a Final, when Peter Reid was upended with the goal in his sights. Sadly, this historic moment overshadowed a wondergoal by Norman Whiteside, who beat the normally reliable Neville Southall from an acute angle just as a replay looked likely. Everton had come to Wembley on the back of the Cup Winners' Cup Final, and had no answer to the Ulsterman's pace: as it turned out, one goal was enough to take the trophy.

As United shot clear of the pack in the early weeks of the 1985-86 season, with ten successive wins and a 15-game unbeaten run, it seemed that at long last the post-

Busby title bogey was about to be laid. But the League is a marathon, not a sprint, and by the time the campaign ended the Red Devils had slumped to fourth. Injuries to Strachan, Robson and promising Dane Jesper Olsen hadn't helped, but in reality there was no excuse for letting a ten-point November lead slip. What was worse, it was Liverpool who were the beneficiaries. Mark Hughes quit for Barcelona at the end of the season and when the following November saw United no longer fourth from top, but fourth from bottom, the writing was on the wall for Big Ron.

After a resounding 4-1 defeat at Southampton in the League Cup, the directors bowed to pressure and showed Atkinson the Old Trafford door. For a replacement, they looked to history by selecting a man who, like Matt Busby, hailed from north of the border. This was a man, too, who would prove significantly more durable than fellow Celt Tommy Docherty. Having taken Aberdeen to European glory in the Cup Winners' Cup, Alex Ferguson was ready to take up the biggest challenge in football. And though his earliest years wouldn't reflect it, he would be the man who finally took the club out of Matt Busby's shadow to create a new golden age.

Below: New signings Mike Phelan and Neil Webb celebrate their arrival at the Theatre of Dreams in 1989.

SBY WAY

Left: Homage to
Sir Matt Busby,
the man whose
reign started
United's success
story.

17

The Club Today

The Alex Ferguson era, which began on 6 November 1986 after a mediocre start to the new season, would turn out to be the modern equivalent of Matt Busby's reign. Indeed, in terms of honours gained over time, it would outshine all competition, though comparisons between different periods of football are always fraught with difficulty.

It may be hard to credit today, though, but Ferguson's position was not always as safe as houses. The end of his second full season in charge, 1988-89, heard the Theatre of Dreams resound to the slow handclap, and it was apparent that fans were no longer prepared to give the 'newcomer' the benefit of the doubt. That he turned the situation around is now glorious history, and – with a contract that takes him through to the year 2000 – Alex is happily an Old Trafford fixture.

When 'Fergie' took the momentous decision to take the hottest seat in the English game, he clearly felt he'd gone as far as he could in Scottish football. His playing career had been spent as a goalscorer for the likes of Dunfermline and Rangers, and there's little doubt he'd have been a prime contender for the Ibrox job had he wanted it. But this complex man, whose managerial record encompassed East Stirling, St Mirren and six years at Aberdeen, was not known for always doing the obvious thing.

He'd been the man the Scottish FA turned to when Jock Stein died of a heart attack on the bench in Cardiff in September 1985. But Fergie ignored the chance to manage

Right: Though rarely seen without a worried frown on his face, manager Alex Ferguson brought a smile to millions of United fans worldwide as his team carried all before them in the 1990s.

Opposite: Gary Pallister was still a mainstay of the United defence in 1997 even though former cohort Steve Bruce had moved on.

Above: Alex Ferguson greets his
admirers

his national team – an opportunity most Scots would give their right arm for – in favour of the Old Trafford job he really wanted. The chance to fulfil that ambition would finally come and the man the directors chose had a track record that was well worth consideration. Ten trophies had arrived at Pittodrie during his reign, making the Fergie era the most successful period in their history. The climax was Aberdeen's first ever European crown, beating Real Madrid to take home the European Cup Winners' Cup.

As previously mentioned, Ferguson's first two Old Trafford seasons didn't set the woods alight, though an FA Cup win in 1990 suggested his massive rebuilding programme – a £4.6 million outlay on Viv Anderson, Steve Bruce, Brian McClair, Mal Donaghy, Jim Leighton and the returning Mark Hughes was boosted by £1.5 million Neil Webb and £750,000 Mike Phelan – had not been a waste of money.

This Cup triumph was achieved after a replay with Crystal Palace, a team managed by Old Trafford old boy Steve Coppell. After a slip by United keeper Leighton had let the underdogs back in at Wembley, Fergie showed steel by replacing him for the replay by Les Sealey, on loan from Luton. Sealey's sure handling ensured that a single goal, from full-back Lee Martin, would prove enough to bring home Fergie's first silverware.

THE FOUNDATION FOR FUTURE SUCCESS

United's fourth attempt to win the Cup Winners' Cup would follow – and away victories at Montpellier (France) and Legia Warsaw (Poland) in the quarter and semi-finals saw them arrive in Rotterdam, hoping to emulate Everton who won the trophy there in 1985. Second-half goals by Mark Hughes against Barcelona, the team he'd briefly left Old Trafford to play for, gave the Reds a 2-1 win.

Off the pitch, United survived an attempt by Michael Knighton to buy out the Edwards family – the second time in five years a sale had looked likely. Previously it had been newspaper tycoon Robert Maxwell who had flashed the cash, and just as he'd turn his attention to Derby after being repulsed, so Knighton would purchase Carlisle United, where he still holds sway today, after the deal collapsed for undisclosed reasons.

Ferguson laid the foundation for future success in August 1989, bringing in Gary Pallister alongside Steve Bruce to form a wonderful central defensive partnership. In midfield, Paul Ince completed an England international trio with Webb and captain Robson keeping the red machine ticking over. After Jim Leighton's apparent fallibility under pressure, a new keeper became a priority – and the August 1991 signing of six foot four inch Danish international Peter Schmeichel added impregnability at the back. (As a happy footnote, Leighton returned north of the border and played well enough to regain his international place with Scotland.)

United's 1991-92 season saw them duel with Leeds United, inspired by Old Trafford old boy Gordon Strachan, for the title. And though they lost out, the Red Devils would snatch Frenchman Eric Cantona from their rivals midway through the following campaign, and he would link with young Welsh winger Ryan Giggs to inspire United to the title. Meanwhile, they ensured the last Division One season would be marked with silverware by bringing home the League Cup with a 1-0 win over Nottingham Forest. Roy Keane, on the losing side that day, would eventually be added to United's staff.

The FA Carling Premiership took a bow at the start of the 1992-93 campaign, and, from the last match of 1992 when they beat Coventry 5-0, United were a constant presence in the top two. Mark Hughes, as ever, had been supplying the goals that stoked the challenge, but it was when Dion Dublin, a £1 million signing from Cambridge, broke his leg against Crystal Palace that Ferguson made his audacious move for Cantona. Leeds slumped to 17th without the Frenchman who, it was rumoured, had fallen out with disciplinarian Howard Wilkinson. Whatever the truth, his recruitment was the catalyst for United's first Championship season. Along with Brian McClair and Ryan Giggs, he'd contributed nine League goals behind top scorer Hughes with 15. The 26-year wait was over…

Alex Ferguson spent heavily to boost his title-winning team, replacing 'Captain Marvel' Bryan Robson (who'd

Left: Known universally as 'Sparky', Welsh forward Mark Hughes' two spells at Old Trafford saw him write his name firmly in United's roll of honour.

Above: The sight of Ryan Giggs flying down the left wing has given delight to United's fans over several seasons, and hopefully will for many more to come.

THE JEWEL IN THE CROWN

United added the FA Cup to their Premiership crown with almost contemptuous ease, emulating Liverpool (in 1985-86), Arsenal (1970-71) and Spurs (1960-61) with a 4-0 dismissal of Chelsea. Eric Cantona made headlines with two penalties in the 60th and 66th minutes, while Paul Ince, 'the Guv'nor', ruled the midfield. The Double, not to mention losing Finalists in the third major competition, was a feat even Matt Busby would have applauded. The late, great manager had passed away in January 1994, and this triumph was dedicated to him.

As United celebrated success, young players like Gary and Philip Neville, David Beckham, Nicky Butt and Paul Scholes prepared to vie for first-team places, leaving Ferguson to buy just one player: David May, a versatile defender who could play equally happily at full-back or centre-half.

The following season saw Eric Cantona make headlines all the way from dismissal in a friendly at Glasgow Rangers to a game on 25 January 1995 at Selhurst Park, home of Crystal Palace. His decision to lash out at full-back Richard Shaw earned him a red card – but it was his response to a foul-mouthed 'fan' as he walked off that would earn him a nine-month FA ban. With Eric went realistic hopes of the title, as Blackburn kept the momentum of the previous season going to pip the Red Devils to top spot in the very last game.

The European Cup had ended with a 3-1 defeat in Gothenburg, where Paul Ince was dismissed for arguing with the referee, There had been problems with the three foreigners rule (now discarded in the wake of the Bosman ruling) which even led Fergie to drop Peter Schmeichel. Such was the emphasis on finding home-born players, that United were driven to break the British transfer record once again in January, when Andy Cole moved from St James' Park to Old Trafford as a potential replacement for the unsettled Mark Hughes.

Last year's Wembley trip had been the icing on the cake, but this time round the FA Cup was United's last chance of a trophy. That hope was dashed by a goal from Paul Rideout after 30 minutes, though the return of Cantona on a new three-year contract (a move to Inter Milan having been rumoured) was a significant silver lining.

Mark Hughes (Chelsea), Paul Ince (Inter Milan) and André Kanchelskis (Everton) all departed in the summer, but United's youngsters – Sharpe, Giggs, Scholes and all – would prove equal to the task of replacing them. Cantona came back and weighed in with some crucial goals, and in March would create an amazing record. Four games brought four goals (no other United player scoring) and ten points thanks to single-goal wins against Newcastle, Arsenal and Tottenham plus a draw at Loftus Road. Eric 'Le God' (as he was dubbed by the fans) was also on target, as United powered their way yet again to the FA Cup Final for the third year running.

There they faced Liverpool, and though the classic match pundits predicted didn't happen, a single Eric strike

played just 14 games) with Roy Keane, creating a British record with a £3.75 million fee. In 1993-94 he'd repay that severalfold as United claimed a second Premiership. By the end of January, United were 16 points clear of second-placed Blackburn.

At one point, an unique treble of League, FA Cup and Coca-Cola Cup seemed on the cards, but the latter saw former Old Trafford supremo Ron Atkinson gain revenge with his then current team Aston Villa and a 3-1 Wembley win. Fergie steadied the United ship as Blackburn cut back their rivals' lead and victory was assured by the last game of the season. Bryan Robson left on a high to take up the Middlesbrough manager's job after 13 years' service.

with just five minutes left proved sufficient to give United a second Double.

Unlike the previous close season, this was to be a summer of acquisition. Paul Parker (Derby) and Steve Bruce (Birmingham) departed, but it was those who arrived at Old Trafford who would make headlines. Many stars had advertised their skills during Euro '96 with Jordi Cruyff and Karel Poborsky impressing Fergie. Central defender Ronny Johnsen came from Besiktas, while Ole Gunnar Solskjaer arrived from Norwegian side Molde.

Newcastle were perceived as United's strongest potential challengers, especially after their strike force had been boosted by the addition of Alan Shearer. It had been an open secret that Fergie would have loved to have brought him to Old Trafford – but when the clubs met in the Charity Shield season-opener, the £15 million England man failed to make the scoresheet, as United raced to a 4-0 victory courtesy of Cantona, Butt, Beckham and Keane.

And it was Beckham who scored the goal of the season on its very first day. The talented young Londoner celebrated his return to the capital with a goal from just inside his own half against Wimbledon, but, as autumn set,

Above left: The imperious figure of Eric Cantona is a sight United learned they would see no more when he announced his shock retirement in 1997.

Above: Andy Cole's United career took time to get going after his record 1995 transfer from Newcastle. Yet a recall to the England squad two years later suggested his return to form had attracted Glenn Hoddle's eye.

THE REAL THING

Alex Ferguson had long ago put the Coca-Cola (League) Cup third on his list of priorities, so defeat to eventual winners Leicester in November was no disaster. But thoughts of a third Double receded in February when, after beating Tottenham, they lost to fellow Londoners Wimbledon by a single goal at Selhurst Park – no repeat of Beckham's opening-day salvo. This also put the pressure on to perform in Europe, and in March Porto were summarily dispatched by a handsome 4-0 margin, the away leg ending goalless.

League results had stuttered back to satisfactory form, two sizeable back-to-back wins against relegation candidates Sunderland (5-0) and Forest (4-0) seeming to clear the creative blockage. From then to the end of the season the Red Devils would lose just two League games, against Derby and, ironically, Sunderland. Andy Cole at last started justifying his huge fee; his Old Trafford stay had been punctuated by injury and illness, and his diligence would see him called up to the England squad at the season's end to replace the unavailable Robbie Fowler.

While some of the imports failed to make the mark that had been predicted – most notably Jordi Cruyff, whose first-team appearances after Black October were few and far between – Solskjaer more than lived up to his Baby-Faced Assassin label, while Johnsen performed quietly but efficiently at the back and reserve keeper Van Der Gouw impressed when required. Even he, though, couldn't stop Borussia Dortmund scoring in the European Cup semi-final via a wicked Pallister deflection. And when the Germans notched the only goal of the return at Old Trafford, it seemed the title would be the only trophy on the table.

Yet a fourth Premiership in five years was certainly nothing to be sniffed at. And even the shock retirement of French superstar Eric Cantona in May 1997 couldn't

United's sunshine football began to lose something of its sparkle. One October week proved the low point of their season, as they went down 5-0 to Newcastle and then 6-3 at Southampton. Even worse, a 40-year unbeaten record at Old Trafford in European competition was next to disappear, as Fenerbahce emerged victorious thanks to a David May own goal. This result left them struggling to reach the knockout stage and a European Cup quarter-final berth, but they achieved it with a 2-0 away win at Rapid Vienna in December.

take the gloss off that. With Ferguson reportedly tabling a bid for Middlesbrough's Juninho as a possible successor and allegedly showing interest in Fiorentina's Argentine hitman Gabriel Batistuta, he clearly wasn't resting on his laurels. And the presence of many United players in the British, Irish and Scandinavian national squads as World Cup qualification games continued through the summer, emphasised that the Manchester United squad was the strongest it had been since the Busby era. Now wasn't that where we came in?

Player Profiles

GOALKEEPERS
Gary Bailey, Peter Schmeichel, Alex Stepney

DEFENDERS
Arthur Albiston, Steve Bruce, Martin Buchan, Bill Foulkes, Denis Irwin, Paul McGrath, Gordon McQueen, Kevin Moran, Gary Neville, Jimmy Nicholl, Gary Pallister.

MIDFIELDERS
David Beckham, Nicky Butt, Steve Coppell, Pat Crerand, Duncan Edwards, Ryan Giggs, Paul Ince, Roy Keane, Brian McClair, Sammy McIlroy, Arnold Muhren, Bryan Robson, Paul Scholes, Lee Sharpe, Nobby Stiles, Gordon Strachan.

STRIKERS
George Best, Eric Cantona, Bobby Charlton, Andy Cole, Mark Hughes, Brian Kidd, Denis Law, Ole Gunnar Solskjaer, Frank Stapleton, Dennis Viollet, Norman Whiteside, Ray Wilkins.

Fantasy Football's been all the rage recently, but any United fan who wants to pick a dream team from the players we've profiled is sure of many selection headaches. United have always boasted a rich selection of quality players, and the 'squad' we've assembled is second to none.

Roles are, of course, a little hazier to define. Is Bobby Charlton a striker or a midfielder – and since Eric Cantona finished 1996-97, his final season as a player, top of the Old Trafford assists table, can he really be called an out and out striker?

Internationals from England, Scotland, Wales, Eire, Holland, Denmark and Norway all feature in these pages, along with European Cup winners, England captains and more, but it's up to you to make the final selection. Before you do so, though, turn the page and find out a little more about the players who've made Old Trafford the Theatre of Dreams.

25

Arthur Albiston

PERSONAL FILE

Born: 14 July 1957
Birthplace: Edinburgh
Height: 5' 7"
Weight: 11st 3lb

LEAGUE RECORD

FROM-TO	CLUB	APPS	GOALS
1974-88	Manchester Utd	379	6
1988-89	West Brom	43	2
1989-90	Dundee	10	—
1990	Chesterfield (loan)	3	1
1991-93	Chester C	68	—
Total		503	9

MANCHESTER UNITED LEAGUE DEBUT

15 October 1974 v Portsmouth

SCOTLAND DEBUT

28 April 1982 v Northern Ireland

SCOTLAND HONOURS

SEASON	CAPS
1981-82	1
1982-83	—
1983-84	5
1984-85	5
1985-86	3
Total	14

DID YOU KNOW?

Arthur's sterling service was honoured in 1988 by a testimonial match against local rivals City that pulled in 15,000 fans.

The maxim 'If you see a chance, take it' could well have been penned for Arthur Albiston, who arrived from his native Edinburgh to join United as an apprentice in 1972. He made his first-team debut, aged just 17, two years later against arch rivals City in a League Cup tie in front of a packed Old Trafford. But it was England's other famous knock-out competition, the FA Cup, that was to prove the stuff of which his dreams were made.

Still only 19, he was called up to replace injured left-back Stewart Houston for the 1977 FA Cup Final against Liverpool and his first appearance in the competition resulted in a winner's medal, as United beat the League Champions 2-1. It was a pivotal point in the young defender's career as he went on to become a regular, if largely unsung, first-team player for ten years.

Quick, nimble and strong in the tackle, Albiston had a sweet left foot and was always happy to turn defence into attack, an ability not unnoticed by Scotland, who capped him at schoolboy, Under-21 and full levels. The peak of his 14-cap international career was a place in the squad for the 1986 World Cup Finals in Mexico.

Albiston lost his place during 1987 and rejoined his old boss Ron Atkinson at West Bromwich the following year, but he departed Old Trafford with 464 appearances in all competitions under his belt. He appeared in four FA Cup Finals, becoming the first United player to win three winner's medals when Everton's dreams of a unique domestic and European treble were shattered by Norman Whiteside's extra-time goal in 1985.

Gary Bailey

PERSONAL FILE

Born: 9 August 1958
Birthplace: Ipswich
Height: 6' 1"
Weight: 13st 2lb

LEAGUE RECORD

FROM-TO	CLUB	APPS	GOALS
1978-87	Manchester Utd	294	—

MANCHESTER UNITED LEAGUE DEBUT

18 November 1978 v Ipswich Town

ENGLAND DEBUT

26 March 1985 v Eire

ENGLAND HONOURS

SEASON	CAPS
1984-85	2
Total	2

DID YOU KNOW?
When West Brom's Tony Brown scored against Gary in December 1978, it was the first time a player had ever scored against a father and son!

A knee injury, sustained while training with the England squad in early 1986, effectively brought the career of Gary Bailey to a cruel end. With the shelf life of a top-class custodian reaching far into a third decade, his loss to football was premature to say the least.

Bailey, the son of ex-Ipswich Town keeper Roy Bailey, moved to South Africa as a youngster, but United spotted his talents playing for Witts University and brought him back to Old Trafford in early 1978. Uncannily, he made his debut against his dad's former club in November and soon made the green jersey his own, going to Wembley the same season only to suffer the heartbreak of losing the FA Cup to Arsenal's last-minute goal.

Success was not to elude Bailey, however, and during a seven-year stint as United's first choice, he was to climb the steps to Wembley's royal box in triumph in 1983 and 1985. England also made use of his talents, capping him at Under-21, B and full levels, though the fact that he gained only two full caps underlined England's overall strength between the sticks.

Gary Bailey's United debut was against his father's club, for whom he could well have been playing had it not been for Eddie Lewis. It was Lewis, a former United star of the 1950s now based in South Africa, who put him on the plane to Old Trafford for a trial. His rival for a place in the side was Chris Turner, but he was undisputed first choice for six out of his eight United seasons. His first term ended in disappointment with FA Cup Final defeat by Arsenal, especially as he might have cut out the cross that led to Alan Sunderland's winner, but he overcame this to show his value to club and country.

A tall, imposing figure, Bailey liked to dominate his area, not unlike his blond counterpart of the present day, Peter Schmeichel. Slightly erratic under the high ball, he atoned time and time again with his agility and his value to the team is demonstrated by a total of 373 first-team appearances in all competitions, which include 20 in Europe. He is currently a leading figure in the South African game, flourishing in that country's new multi-racial society.

1993-1997

David Beckham

PERSONAL FILE

Born: 2 May 1975
Birthplace: Leytonstone
Height: 6' 0"
Weight: 11st 2lb

LEAGUE RECORD

FROM-TO	CLUB	APPS	GOALS
1993-97	Manchester Utd	73	15
1994-95	Preston (loan)	5	2
Total		78	17

MANCHESTER UNITED LEAGUE DEBUT

2 April 1995 v Leeds United

ENGLAND DEBUT

1 September 1996 v Moldova

ENGLAND HONOURS (TO 31 MAY 1997)

SEASON	CAPS
1996-97	7
Total	7

STAR QUOTE

'His goal against Wimbledon was the best I've seen in my life. It will never be bettered.'
MATTHEW LE TISSIER

28

David Beckham's rise to prominence in English football has been little short of meteoric – so much so that Old Trafford regulars already feel inclined to mention the midfielder in the same breath as Edwards, Charlton and Best. He looks destined to be a United captain and is an established part of the England squad, having already won two Premiership titles including one Double. All this from someone who only turned 22 in May 1997.

Born in Leytonstone, London, Beckham is a product of the Sir Bobby Charlton Soccer School and his strong affinity for the club saw him join United as a schoolboy in June 1989, despite overtures from most of the top London clubs.

Part of United's brilliant Youth Cup-winning side of 1992, he made his debut as a substitute at Brighton in a League Cup tie in September of the same year.

After an initial period of bedding-in, which included a loan spell at Preston, Beckham began to make his presence felt in the first team during the 1995-96 season and was soon a vital component in United's powerful squad. League and Cup honours were his reward and a magnificent season was capped by his inclusion in Glenn Hoddle's first England squad for the World Cup qualifier against Moldova.

Beckham's 1996-97 season started on a high with his dramatic goal from the half-way line in the opening fixture against Wimbledon. The audacious chip that beat Neil Sullivan all ends up could have made the rest of the campaign an anti-climax – but as one local radio reporter said 'it was the fact he kept his standards up all season long that was the bonus for United.'

For England, too: far from being a fringe player, he stepped confidently into his country's established team, playing Le Tournoi in the summer of 1997, and on returning home found that he would be the man to take the departed Eric Cantona's Number 7 shirt, new boy Teddy Sheringham adopting his earlier Number 10. It took a big talent to fill the shirt of 'Eric Le God', but at Old Trafford there was none bigger.

Imaginative and creative, Beckham's distribution is first class and his 'engine' high-powered. His strong-running forays, culminating in powerful shooting with either foot, have drawn comparisons with Charlton, and his dead-ball free-kicks are feared throughout football. Composed beyond his years, he will become a formidable opponent on any stage as he strengthens and is destined to become an integral part of England's World Cup challenge in 1998.

'I am quite a confident person, but I do get nervous…the nerves last about five minutes then I relax.'

George Best

PERSONAL FILE

Born: 22 May 1946
Birthplace: Belfast
Height: 5' 8"
Weight: 10st 3lb

LEAGUE RECORD

FROM-TO	CLUB	APPS	GOALS
1963-74	Manchester Utd	361	137
1975	Stockport (loan)	3	2
1976-78	LA Aztecs	55	27
1976-77	Fulham	42	8
1978-79	Fort Lauderdale	28	6
1980-81	San Jose	56	21
1983	Bournemouth	5	—
Total		550	201

MANCHESTER UNITED LEAGUE DEBUT

14 September 1963 v West Bromwich Albion

NORTHERN IRELAND DEBUT

15 April 1964 v Wales

NORTHERN IRELAND HONOURS

SEASON	CAPS
1963-64	2
1964-65	7
1965-66	3
1966-67	1
1967-68	1
1968-69	4
1969-70	4
1970-71	6
1971-72	2
1972-73	1
1973-74	1
1974-75	—
1975-76	—
1976-77	3
1977-78	2
Total	37

STAR QUOTE

'You can never replace the buzz of 60,000 people screaming your name when you've stuck three in the back of the net.'

If any one player typifies both the glamour and the worldwide acclaim of Manchester United it is George Best, the shy, homesick Belfast boy who blossomed into the most famous, and arguably greatest, footballing talent the British Isles ever produced.

Plucked from obscurity at 15 by Matt Busby, Best found it difficult to settle in England but eventually came to terms with the switch with the combined help of the fatherly Scot and fellow Irishman Harry Gregg. Busby, who saw the spirit of his tragic Babes in Best, blooded his 'Boy Wonder' at 17 against West Bromwich Albion in September 1963 and the young wing wizard went on to play 26 times that season, winning an international debut for Northern Ireland soon after. A legend was born.

Championship honours followed in the 1964-65 season, by which time Best was front-page news. Young, glamorous and successful, he set trends in fashion and hairstyles off the pitch and bewildered opponents on it with his sublime skills. Breathtaking ball control, searing pace and the strength of a natural athlete, made Best a feared rival. Brilliant in the air for a relatively small man, he had few equals in front of goal and was hailed as possibly the most complete player in the world.

With his greatest season yet to come, what could possibly go wrong?

In 1967-68, defending Champions United could only finish second – but their finest hour came at Wembley in May 1968 when, inspired by Best's wonderful solo goal, they beat Benfica 4-1 to be crowned European Cup winners. George ended the season with 32 goals, the Footballer of the Year trophy and the prestigious European Player of the Year award. But the disruptive side of the genius was already beginning to surface, and when Busby stepped down in 1969 the most influential figure vanished from Best's life.

After years of public squabbling over drinking bouts, non-appearances and domestic upheavals, Best finally walked out of Old Trafford for good in 1974 having scored 178 goals in 466 games in all competitions. His comparative absence from the international scene – just 37 caps and no World Cup Finals – remains something of a travesty to his talent. A self-declared alcoholic, Best had forgettable comeback spells with a host of clubs but will always be remembered as one of the world's great footballing stars.

In 1997, he was still in demand as a football pundit on Sky TV.

Steve Bruce

PERSONAL FILE

Born: 31 December 1960
Birthplace: Newcastle
Height: 6' 0"
Weight: 13st 0lb

LEAGUE RECORD

FROM-TO	CLUB	APPS	GOALS
1978-84	Gillingham	205	29
1984-87	Norwich C	141	14
1987-96	Manchester Utd	309	36
1996-97	Birmingham C	32	—
Total		687	79

MANCHESTER UNITED LEAGUE DEBUT

19 December 1987 v Portsmouth

ENGLAND DEBUT

N/A

ENGLAND HONOURS

None (England Youth only)

STAR QUOTE

'It was the biggest thrill of the lot to find out United wanted me. I needed a slap in the face to realise it was true.'

Rejected by several professional clubs as a young midfielder, Newcastle-born Steve Bruce finally found a footballing home in the south of England at Third Division Gillingham. This dogged perseverance was to become a large part of his make-up, as he fought his way up from unpromising beginnings to become one of Manchester United's most successful captains.

Bruce, fashioned into a central defender at Gillingham, left for Norwich City in 1984 after more than 200 appearances and lifted the Football League Cup with them in 1985 before winning the Second Division Championship the following season. Alex Ferguson decided he was just the man to add steel to United's back four and splashed out £825,000 in December 1987.

Given his debut against Portsmouth, Bruce suffered the first of many broken noses playing in the famous red shirt and his never-say-die attitude found an immediate place in fans' hearts. Tough and combative, Bruce's barrel-chested approach typified United under Ferguson and major honours were just around the corner.

He scored an amazing 16 goals in all competitions (including ten penalties) from the centre of defence, as United won the Cup Winners' Cup after their 1990 FA Cup triumph over Crystal Palace had given them a route into Europe.

League Cup honours followed 12 months later, but Steve's proudest moment

came in 1993 when he became the first Reds captain in 26 years to lift the League title.

The backbone of the side alongside Gary Pallister, Bruce (surprisingly never capped at full level by England) skippered United to their first Double in 1994. He did likewise for the majority of their historic second Double season in 1995-96, though he struggled for his place towards the end after being injured. He left for Birmingham soon after, having played 407 games.

Martin Buchan

PERSONAL FILE

Born: 6 March 1949
Birthplace: Aberdeen
Height: 5' 10"
Weight: 12st 6lb

LEAGUE RECORD

FROM-TO	CLUB	APPS	GOALS
1966-72	Aberdeen	133	8
1972-83	Manchester Utd	376	4
1983-84	Oldham Ath	28	—
Total		537	12

MANCHESTER UNITED LEAGUE DEBUT

4 March 1972 v Tottenham Hotspur

SCOTLAND DEBUT

13 October 1971 v Portugal

SCOTLAND HONOURS

SEASON	CAPS
1971-72	6
1972-73	3
1973-74	6
1974-75	3
1975-76	2
1976-77	5
1977-78	6
1978-79	3
Total	34

DID YOU KNOW?

Martin's total of four goals in 445 games (in all competitions) must make him one of United's all-time lowest scorers.

In terms of value for money, Martin Buchan must rank as one of United's shrewdest-ever purchases, secured from Aberdeen for just £125,000 in 1972 by much-maligned manager Frank O'Farrell. Buchan was about to turn 23 when he arrived at Old Trafford, but he had already captained his former club to Scottish Cup glory, been voted his country's Footballer of the Year and won full international honours.

A natural leader, he combined almost telepathic positional play with a deceptive pace to outwit his opponents. An old head on young shoulders, he immediately instilled a calm authority in United's defence and was one of the first names on the teamsheet for 11 years.

Rather unfortunately for Buchan in terms of success, his time at the club coincided with Liverpool's domination of the domestic scene. Yet he captained Tommy Docherty's side to a victory at Wembley in 1977 that prevented a League, FA Cup and European Cup Treble for the Merseysiders. Buchan thereby became the first player since the war to captain English and Scottish Cup-winning sides.

In later years, Buchan was dogged by injuries and after over 450 games for the club left for Oldham Athletic on a free transfer in 1983.

However, after a season spent fighting off relegation, a troublesome thigh problem signalled the end of a playing career which had seen him represent Scotland 34 times.

A subsequent spell in charge of Burnley quickly convinced Buchan he was not the managerial type, and he left football to pursue a career promoting sports goods.

Nicky Butt

PERSONAL FILE

Born: 21 January 1975
Birthplace: Manchester
Height: 5' 10"
Weight: 11st 3lb

LEAGUE RECORD

FROM-TO	CLUB	APPS	GOALS
1992-97	Manchester Utd	82	8

MANCHESTER UNITED LEAGUE DEBUT

21 November 1992 v Oldham Athletic

ENGLAND DEBUT

29 March 1997 v Mexico

ENGLAND HONOURS (TO 31 MAY 1997)

SEASON	CAPS
1996-97	2
Total	2

DID YOU KNOW?
Before Bryan Robson quit Old Trafford, he accurately predicted Nicky would be the player who would one day fill his boots for club and country.

Another graduate of United's feted youth policy – lately dubbed 'Fergie's Fledglings' – Nicky Butt is, at 22, an accomplished part of a powerful squad that will again challenge for European Champions' League honours in 1997-98. Butt, on the small side at five foot ten and 11 stone, belies his frame with a ferocious tackle and will to win second to none.

Graduating from the same youth side as David Beckham, he has watched his team-mate race ahead of him in terms of international recognition but has become a regular alongside him in Glenn Hoddle's squad. At home, his contribution to the 1995-96 Double season was warmly regarded.

In fact, Butt has packed a lifetime's achievement into his young career and it is testimony to United's multi-talented outfit that his role in the 1996-97 Championship side was mainly unsung. A Youth Cup winner in 1992, he also played for England Under-19s in the 1993 World Cup in Australia, having made his United debut late the previous year against Oldham. Injuries during 1994-95 saw Butt thrust into the limelight, and his impressive displays against the likes of Barcelona and Gothenburg in the European Cup marked him as a future England international.

Competing with Roy Keane for the anchor role in the midfield slowed Butt's progress somewhat in 1997, but the Manchester-born battler has time on his side. A strong-running performer with a fierce right-foot shot, Butt's game will be almost complete when his ball distribution matches his endeavour.

Eric Cantona

LEAGUE RECORD

FROM-TO	CLUB	APPS	GOALS
1983-85	Auxerre	13	2
1985-86	Martigues	—	—
1986-88	Auxerre	68	21
1988-89	Marseille	22	5
1989	Bordeaux	11	6
1989-90	Montpellier	33	10
1990-91	Marseille	18	8
1991-92	Nimes	17	2
1992	Leeds Utd	28	9
1992-97	Manchester Utd	143	64
Total		353	127

MANCHESTER UNITED LEAGUE DEBUT

6 December 1992 v Manchester City

FRANCE HONOURS

Was capped 45 times by his country.

STAR QUOTE

'When seagulls follow the trawler, it is because they think that sardines will be thrown into the sea.'

The enfant terrible of enfant terribles has possibly had more impact on the destiny of the English Championship over the past five years than any other single player. Cantona joined Leeds from Nimes for £900,000, making six starts and nine substitute appearances as Howard Wilkinson's team was confirmed as 1992 League Champions.

But after scoring six goals in 13 games at the start of their title defence, Cantona, clearly not happy, moved on to Manchester United for £1.2 million. Four Championships later, Alex Ferguson and United are eternally grateful.

Cantona's ability to drop off defenders and find space, to dictate the pace of a game, to score crucial goals and, primarily, to make passes that mere mortals wouldn't even dream about, undoubtedly led United's renaissance. But the flip side, including fines and suspensions as he played for six different clubs in France, was not so pretty.

At Old Trafford, Cantona contributed nine goals in 22 games for the first Championship in 1993, 18 in 34 in 1994. But still the dark shadows emerged, with a fine and several red cards, before he topped all previous indiscretions by leaping into the crowd in 1995 to kung-fu kick a Crystal Palace supporter.

Cantona was out of football for eight months, fleeing to France and considering a move to Inter Milan. But his registration remained with United and he returned in triumph, scoring on his first game back in a 2-2 draw with Liverpool. He collected just one yellow card in his first 21 games back as United caught and then overhauled Newcastle. He also played a part as United retained their title in 1996-97, but in May, days after the job was done, he announced his retirement from the game. United owed him much, and the feeling was hopefully mutual.

It was asking too much of anyone to aim to fill the boots and Number 7 shirt of the departed genius, but Teddy Sheringham, United's major summer signing of 1997, was certainly intending to do the former – even if he insisted on keeping the Number 10 he traditionally wears for club and country. David Beckham, it was announced, would wear the Number 7 in future.

'He is capable of producing things with his vision and touch…he lifts everyone round about him.'
ALEX FERGUSON

1954-1973

Bobby Charlton

STAR QUOTE

'I love adventure, and I would like to see a return to the type of football we thrived on in our prime.'

If Manchester United is a name known and respected throughout the world, then Bobby Charlton is surely the jewel in their crown. A survivor of Munich, he came back to win the World Cup with England in 1966 and the European Cup two years later, all the while establishing a reputation for excellence and sportsmanship few at any club can rival.

He burst onto the scene in 1956-57, scoring ten goals in his first 14 League appearances, and by 1958-59, when he notched 29 in 38, was a mainstay of the side. His forte was the solo run, shimmying past opposition and striding out towards goal before unleashing a trademark blockbuster with either foot – and this was a trait that continued even when he moved back into midfield as the years advanced.

He shone for England, too, playing in three World Cups (1962, 1966 and 1970), clocking up 106 caps and breaking Billy Wright's long-standing record (since overtaken, of course, by Peter Shilton). In England's World Cup-winning year, Bobby was voted both England's and Europe's Player of the Year.

Charlton had come from the finest footballing stock. Brother Jack, a rugged central defender for Leeds, was also a World Cup hero, while their uncle, the legendary Newcastle striker Jackie Milburn, was from a notable family that also

produced footballing cousins George, James and John.

Charlton's announcement in 1973 that he was to retire at the end of the current campaign sparked the highest League attendance of the season, and his loss was one that could not easily be replaced: it was hardly a coincidence that relegation followed hard on his departure.

His record of a goal in every three games was as impressive as his career in management would be mundane: a spell at Preston saw him re-register as a player in 1974, clearly feeling he could still do a job at a lower level of football, but he resigned as manager on a point of principle in August 1975.

Despite this, Sir Bobby Charlton (he was knighted in 1994) remains a legend of both United and English football. Since sensibly leaving management to his brother Jack, he's taken his place on United's board and continues as an ambassador for United and football worldwide.

Andy Cole

PERSONAL FILE

Born: 15 October 1971
Birthplace: Nottingham
Height: 5' 11"
Weight: 11st 2lb

LEAGUE RECORD

FROM-TO	CLUB	APPS	GOALS
1989-92	Arsenal	1	—
1991-92	Fulham (loan)	13	3
1992	Bristol C (loan)	12	8
1992-93	Bristol C	29	12
1993-95	Newcastle Utd	70	55
1995-97	Manchester Utd	62	30
Total		187	108

MANCHESTER UNITED LEAGUE DEBUT

22 January 1995 v Blackburn Rovers

ENGLAND DEBUT

29 March 1995 v Uruguay

ENGLAND HONOURS (TO 31 MAY 1997)

SEASON	CAPS
1994-95	1
1995-96	—
1996-97	—
Total	1

STAR QUOTE

'It gets lonely up there on your own sometimes...especially if you're getting hammered. But you've got to dig deep.'

Every successful manager can tell the tale of the one that got away. For George Graham, the man who brought trophies galore to Highbury in his inspirational nine years in charge, ditching goal merchant Andy Cole remains his major misjudgement of a player.

The forward was initially just one of several promising youngsters to roll off Arsenal's youth production line. After graduating from the FA's National School of Excellence at Lilleshall, Cole found himself behind the likes of Campbell and Merson as Graham's team won the Championship in 1989 and 1991. Cole made only one League appearance for the Gunners, as sub in December 1990 at Sheffield United.

The next autumn Cole was farmed out to Fulham, where he struck three times in 13 Second Division games. Cole then went on loan to Bristol City, scoring eight goals in 12 Division One games at the end of the 1991-92 season, and manager Denis Smith gambled £500,000 in July to make the move permanent.

Cole started the 1992-93 season in hot form at Ashton Gate and, after 12 goals in 29 League games, Kevin Keegan shocked the football world – not for the last time in Andy Cole transfer deals – by paying out a club record £1.75 million in March 1993.

It was, of course, a masterstroke. Cole grabbed a goal a game in the 12-match run-in, as Newcastle clinched the Endsleigh League Championship and a place in the top flight. Cole peaked the next season as the Magpies stormed to third place in the Premiership thanks to 41 goals (34 coming in 40 League games) in a game-plan centred around Cole's acceleration into space and unerring eye for goal.

The following season brought criticism as well as plaudits, but Cole had still notched nine goals in 18 League games when he was sold to Manchester United for an English record of £7 million (including Keith Gillespie moving in part exchange). The football world was staggered, and Cole, making his United debut in a 1-0 win over

Blackburn on 22 January 1995, did well to score 12 times in the final 18 Premiership games. He also made his England debut in the friendly against Uruguay.

With Keegan spending £6 million on Les Ferdinand as Cole's replacement, Newcastle led United for much of the 1995-96 season, the former Arsenal apprentice proving less prolific than before. His all-round game, linking with the brilliance of Cantona and Giggs, had improved, but a frequent scowl on the face showed the price to be paid for multi-million pound stardom. At the age of 25, however, the best could yet be ahead.

1975-1983

Steve Coppell

PERSONAL FILE

Born: 9 July 1955
Birthplace: Liverpool
Height: 5' 6"
Weight: 10st 3lb

LEAGUE RECORD

FROM-TO	CLUB	APPS	GOALS
1974-75	Tranmere R	38	10
1975-83	Manchester Utd	322	54
Total		360	64

MANCHESTER UNITED LEAGUE DEBUT

1 March 1975 v Cardiff City

ENGLAND DEBUT

16 November 1977 v Italy

ENGLAND HONOURS

SEASON	CAPS
1977-78	7
1978-79	9
1979-80	9
1980-81	8
1981-82	7
1982-83	2
Total	42

DID YOU KNOW?
Steve Coppell was briefly the 15th Maine Road manager since Joe Mercer – if you count Malcolm Allison twice!

Few United supporters had heard of Steve Coppell when, in early 1975, Tommy Docherty paid Third Division Tranmere Rovers £40,000 for the Liverpool University graduate, stealing the young winger from under the noses of Liverpool and Everton.

Ironically, it had been recently retired Liverpool manager Bill Shankly, helping Tranmere Rovers with a few scouting tips, who had insisted his old club should run the rule over a player making a name for himself in their own backyard. They took no notice, so he gave fellow Scot Docherty a call, and Coppell was soon linking with Irishman Gerry Daly, in a new-look United midfield.

The Stretford End was soon singing the praises of the raw-boned 19-year-old, whose pillaging style down United's right flank, culminating in vicious crosses or rasping drives, had defenders quaking in their boots. Coppell was soon a first-team regular, and found instant success as relegated United bounced straight back to the top flight as Champions.

Coppell's wing raids, perfectly complemented the following season by the equally direct Gordon Hill, promised exciting times for United and so it proved, as three FA Cup Finals resulted in a winner's medal in 1977. Undertaking a more restrained role for Dave Sexton, Coppell played 206 consecutive League games in the late 1970s and early 1980s and made his England debut in 1977, becoming a regular on the international scene. But disaster struck in 1983 when, after a series of operations to correct a badly damaged knee, he was forced to quit football at just 28. He had made nearly 400 appearances for United in all competitions, scoring 70 goals, and been capped 42 times.

A month before his 29th birthday in June 1984, Coppell became the youngest-ever League manager when taking over at Crystal Palace and he took them to the First Division and an FA Cup Final, where they were beaten by none other than his old club.

He resigned when Palace lost their Premiership status in 1993 but, after a series of administrative roles and an ill-fated short spell as Manchester City boss in 1996, he returned to Selhurst Park and guided them back to the Premiership via the play-offs in 1997.

Despite nearly a decade of service, Steve only won one medal – a 1977 FA Cup winner's – missing the 1983 Final through injury.

Pat Crerand

PERSONAL FILE

Born: 19 February 1939
Birthplace: Glasgow
Height: 5' 10"
Weight: 12st 1lb

LEAGUE RECORD

FROM-TO	CLUB	APPS	GOALS
1957-63	Celtic	91	4
1963-71	Manchester Utd	304	10
Total		395	14

MANCHESTER UNITED LEAGUE DEBUT

23 February 1963 v Blackpool

SCOTLAND DEBUT

3 May 1961 v Eire

SCOTLAND HONOURS

SEASON	CAPS
1960-61	3
1961-62	6
1962-63	2
1963-64	1
1964-65	3
1965-66	1
Total	16

Born in the feared Gorbals area of Glasgow, Pat Crerand was bound for a career in the city's feted shipbuilding industry until signed to Celtic's books in 1957. Cast in the mould of the liners his old pals would send out into the Clyde, the rugged Scot forged the role later to be enjoyed by the likes of Paul Ince and Roy Keane.

But it would be unfair to overlook the creative part of Crerand's game, which extended far beyond the ability to merely blunt rival teams' attacks. Plucked from Celtic for around £55,000 after six seasons at Parkhead, he could look extremely elegant on the ball and would spray passes the length and breadth of the pitch. However, his reputation was built largely on his aggressive tackling and a fearsome temper which often landed him in hot water.

His transfer was hailed by the Daily Mail as a masterstroke, even though United already had a surfeit of wing-halves in Jimmy Nicholson, Nobby Lawton, skipper Maurice Setters and Nobby Stiles.

'Manager Matt Busby has tried permutations from all four in the past two seasons, but wing-half has proved his most persistent headache. Crerand has the experience, the temperament and the football to solve it.'

A Wembley FA Cup winner just three months after arriving at Old Trafford, Crerand went on to win two League Championship medals in 1965 and 1967 and was part of the most famous United team of all, the 1968 European Cup-winning side. He played the best part of 400 games for the club in all competitions, a tally of 15 goals underselling his ability, and represented his country 16 times in an age when Scotland was graced by numerous world-class half-backs.

After a spell on the Old Trafford coaching staff, including a period as assistant manager, Crerand held a short-lived post as Northampton boss in the mid 1970s but is now divorced from the game. Still highly respected, he is always called upon for an opinion by the media when United are making the headlines.

DID YOU KNOW?

In 1961 Pat claimed he wouldn't leave Parkhead 'for England, Italy or anywhere in the world...even if they gave me £10,000.' But Busby knew better!

1953-1958

Duncan Edwards

PERSONAL FILE

Born: 1 October 1936
Died: 21 February 1958
Birthplace: Dudley
Height: 5' 11"
Weight: 13st 0lb

LEAGUE RECORD

FROM-TO	CLUB	APPS	GOALS
1953-58	Manchester Utd	151	20

MANCHESTER UNITED LEAGUE DEBUT

4 April 1953 v Cardiff City

ENGLAND DEBUT

2 April 1955 v Scotland

ENGLAND HONOURS

SEASON	CAPS
1954-55	4
1955-56	5
1956-57	6
1957-58	3
Total	18

STAR QUOTE

'If I had to play for my life, and could take one man with me, it would be Duncan.'
BOBBY CHARLTON

Among the many great names who have passed the through the ranks at Old Trafford, Duncan Edwards stands supreme. Like rock'n'roll hero Buddy Holly, who died in a plane crash mere months after Munich, Edwards stands as a talent cut off in its prime, an icon of English football at its brightest and best.

At just 21 years of age, it's not inconceivable he could have remained a first-team regular for the decade that would end with United taking the trophy they had been pursuing with such intent when the fated airliner failed to leave German soil. More than that, many still believe he could well have captained England to World Cup glory in place of 1966 hero Bobby Moore.

Though United lost on his debut against Cardiff, his only match that season, Edwards' talent was soon manifest, and at 18 years and 183 days he was the youngest person ever to represent his country at full level when selected for the 1955 Home Internationals. In the four seasons to come before his untimely passing he'd take his total of caps to 18.

Though not a prolific scorer, Edwards could bulge the net with either foot, and once scored a hat-trick for England's Under-23 side against Scotland. He'd typically wear the left-half's Number 6 shirt, indicating a more withdrawn midfield role, but would link with another great talent, left-back Roger Byrne, to set up attacks. His

four full seasons in United's first team brought two League Championship medals and a losing FA Cup Final appearance.

In a team of greats, Edwards was the outstanding talent. United assistant manager Jimmy Murphy termed him 'the Kohinoor diamond amongst our crown jewels'. His talents are celebrated in his home town of Dudley where the parish church of St Francis contains a stained glass window dedicated to his memory.

41

Bill Foulkes

PERSONAL FILE

Born: 5 January 1932
Birthplace: St Helens
Height: 5' 11"
Weight: 12st 4lb

LEAGUE RECORD

FROM-TO	CLUB	APPS	GOALS
1951-70	Manchester Utd	566	7

MANCHESTER UNITED LEAGUE DEBUT

13 December 1952 v Liverpool

ENGLAND DEBUT

2 October 1954 v Northern Ireland

ENGLAND HONOURS

SEASON	CAPS
1954-55	1
Total	1

DID YOU KNOW?

Bill's medal collection was sold for £37,000 at Christie's in 1992: a reminder that footballers weren't always as well paid as today.

Bill Foulkes is not a name that rolls readily off the tongue of the uninitiated. Yet, like his revered team-mate Bobby Charlton, he survived the Munich air disaster in 1958 to perpetuate the dream of the Busby Babes and bring the European Cup back to Old Trafford a decade later.

Foulkes, a man the fans claimed was quarried rather than conceived, was born of mining stock in St Helens in 1932 and was discovered playing for Whiston Boys Club in 1949, turning professional two years later. Once in the team at the turn of 1953, he remained a first choice for 18 seasons.

Four Championships, an FA Cup winner's medal and that historic European success, as captain, are just reward for his consistency. When he bowed out in 1970, Bill Foulkes had made an incredible 679 appearances for the Reds, a total bettered only by Charlton.

A superb header of the ball and physically imposing despite being under six foot, Foulkes became the defensive rock on which Matt Busby built after the cruel decimation of his team in 1958. He skippered the makeshift side beaten by Bolton in the FA Cup Final of that year, and proved invaluable as United painstakingly rebuilt their empire.

Foulkes played just once for England, and this less than two years after his United debut. It was at right-back, the position he first adopted at Old Trafford before moving to the centre of the defence, and the game against Northern Ireland ended in a 2-0 win.

Foulkes played alongside some of the best players ever to grace Old Trafford, from the tragic Duncan Edwards and Tommy Taylor to Charlton, Law and Best. A coach in America, Norway and Japan in later years, he remains the epitome of Manchester United under Busby.

1990-1997

Ryan Giggs

PERSONAL FILE

Born: 29 November 1973
Birthplace: Cardiff
Height: 5' 11"
Weight: 10st 7lb

LEAGUE RECORD

FROM-TO	CLUB	APPS	GOALS
1990-97	Manchester Utd	207	42

MANCHESTER UNITED LEAGUE DEBUT

2 March 1991 v Everton

WALES DEBUT

16 October 1991 v West Germany

WALES HONOURS (TO 31 MAY 1997)

SEASON	CAPS
1991-92	3
1992-93	5
1993-94	3
1994-95	2
1995-96	3
1996-97	3
Total	19

STAR QUOTE
'He makes you believe there is a football God after all.'
RON ATKINSON

Rarely can a young player have made such an impression on the football world as Ryan Giggs, the precocious 17-year-old who, having come on against Everton, scored the winning goal of the Manchester derby in his first full game. Comparisons with the legendary George Best were inevitable and it is to his credit that Giggs has remained even-headed, given the level of success he has enjoyed.

Refusing to rush the young Welsh winger, Alex Ferguson used Giggs intermittently after his extraordinary 1991 introduction, but, by the following year, his marvellous displays made it a crime to exclude him. Running at top pace with the ball seemingly glued to his feet, shimmying past defender after defender before blasting the ball home with his sorcerer's-wand of a left foot, Giggs was voted Young Player of the Year at the end of his first campaign in 1992. That season, he had come off the bench to become Wales' youngest-ever full cap at 17 years and 321 days.

Giggs, Young Player of the Year again in 1993, won his first Championship that year and 12 months later was a Double winner at just 20 years of age. Some would say his dip in form as United surrendered the title the following season was inevitable, but he bounced back to win an incredible second Double and yet another Championship in 1997.

The achievements of Giggs, who, at the time of writing, is still only 23, are difficult to comprehend. A slight criticism is his lack of goals in the past few seasons, but this can be attributed to United's emergence as a complete team unit comprising 11 gifted individuals. If, as expected, he takes over the pivotal role enjoyed of late by Eric Cantona, we can expect Giggs' free-flowing, direct style to return and there are no limits to his aspirations.

1980-1986 & 1988-1995

Mark Hughes

PERSONAL FILE

Born: 1 November 1963
Birthplace: Wrexham
Height: 5' 9"
Weight: 13st 5lb

LEAGUE RECORD

FROM-TO	CLUB	APPS	GOALS
1980-86	Manchester Utd	89	37
1986-87	Barcelona	28	4
1987-88	Bayern Munich (loan)	18	6
1988-95	Manchester Utd	256	82
1995-97	Chelsea	66	16
Total		457	145

MANCHESTER UNITED LEAGUE DEBUT

21 January 1984 v Southampton

WALES DEBUT

2 May 1984 v England

WALES HONOURS (TO 31 MAY 1997)

SEASON	CAPS
1983-84	2
1984-85	7
1985-86	3
1986-87	2
1987-88	6
1988-89	5
1989-90	3
1990-91	7
1991-92	8
1992-93	7
1993-94	3
1994-95	4
1995-96	3
1996-97	5
Total	65

DID YOU KNOW?
Mark was signed for Barcelona by Terry Venables.

Few would argue that Mark Hughes is among the greatest all-round forwards Britain has ever produced, and he has a medals tally to match. On the small side at five foot nine, he makes up for his lack of height with an incredible body strength which enables him to shield the ball better than any player in living memory. Lethal in the air and possessor of uncanny volleying skills, Hughes, now with Chelsea, remains at 33 a world-class striker.

'Sparky' leapt onto the first team stage at 20 with a goal on his debut against Oxford in a 1983 League Cup tie, an achievement he was to repeat when he made his international bow the following year against England in his home town of Wrexham. In his first full season, Hughes picked up an FA Cup winner's medal and the Young Player of the Year award after scoring 24 goals. Suddenly a wanted man, he was sold to Barcelona in 1986 for around £2 million, to the anger and disappointment of fans.

Things did not work out, however, and, after a loan spell at Bayern Munich, Hughes arrived back at Old Trafford in 1988.

His physical style had not found favour with Spanish referees – 'my aggression got me into trouble,' he said, 'even when I didn't do anything wrong' – and it was only when that canny coach Uli Hoeness at Bayern put his career back on the rails that the old Mark Hughes shone through once more.

Confidence restored, he picked up where he had left off and his part in United's re-emergence cannot be underestimated. By the time Hughes departed a second time in 1995, he had picked up two Championships and a further two FA Cups, including a Double, a League Cup and possibly his sweetest moment when scoring the two goals that sank old team-mates Barcelona in the 1991 European Cup Winners' Cup Final.

In two spells at United he made 449 appearances, scoring 162 goals. Twice the PFA's Player of the Year, Hughes became the only player this century to win four FA Cup winner's medals, as he helped Chelsea triumph over relegation-bound Middlesbrough in May 1997.

'I'd like people to remember me as a
          hard worker who always gave my all –
not a dirty so-and-so.'

Paul Ince

PERSONAL FILE

Born: 21 October 1967
Birthplace: Ilford
Height: 5' 10"
Weight: 12st 2lb

LEAGUE RECORD

FROM-TO	CLUB	APPS	GOALS
1985-89	West Ham Utd	72	7
1989-95	Manchester Utd	206	24
1995-97	Inter Milan	n/k	n/k
Total		278	31

MANCHESTER UNITED LEAGUE DEBUT

16 September 1989 v Millwall

ENGLAND DEBUT

9 September 1992 v Spain

ENGLAND HONOURS (TO 31 MAY 1997)

SEASON	CAPS
1992-93	9
1993-94	5
1994-95	2
1995-96	7
1996-97	7
Total	30

Following a slow start exacerbated by an acrimonious, drawn-out parting from West Ham in 1989, £2 million purchase Paul Ince evolved from a promising Cockney midfielder into the driving force behind Manchester's United's climb to the summit of English football in the early 1990s.

Ince overcame a difficult childhood, which saw his father leave home when he was still a toddler and his mother relocate to Germany when he was 11. He's always credited West Ham manager John Lyall with keeping him on the straight and narrow as he grew up in London's tough East End. 'I owe John so much,' confessed Ince, who revealed that had Lyall not been sacked he himself might have stayed at Upton Park.

More of a ball-player for the London club, Alex Ferguson saw Ilford-born Ince as a new Bryan Robson, and set about channelling his aggression towards the good of the team. Along with Robson, Steve Bruce and Mark Hughes, Ince added the steel to a United side filled with attacking talent, and success came quickly with winner's medals in the FA Cup and European Cup Winners' Cup in successive seasons.

His strong running from deep positions and vital goals played a huge part in bringing the title back to Old Trafford in 1993 after an absence of a quarter of a century, and Ince was the pillar of strength as United landed their first domestic Double the following season.

By this time his international career had really taken off. First picked by Graham Taylor in 1992, Ince became the first black player to captain England the following year. He seemed destined to be a cornerstone for club and country for years to come, but – after United lost the title to Blackburn in 1995 – he was surprisingly sold to Inter Milan for £8 million.

A losing UEFA Cup Finalist in 1997, Ince was consistently rumoured to be considering a return to the Premiership for the 1997-98 season.

STAR QUOTE

'We were the top team in Manchester while I was there – now I've moved, I'll be trying to make AC Milan the Man City and Inter the Man Utd.'

1990-1997

Denis Irwin

PERSONAL FILE

Born: 31 October 1965
Birthplace: Cork
Height: 5' 8"
Weight: 10st 8lb

LEAGUE RECORD

FROM-TO	CLUB	APPS	GOALS
1983-86	Leeds Utd	72	1
1986-90	Oldham Ath	167	4
1990-97	Manchester Utd	256	15
Total		495	20

MANCHESTER UNITED LEAGUE DEBUT

25 August 1990 v Coventry City

EIRE DEBUT

12 September 1990 v Morocco

EIRE HONOURS (TO 31 MAY 1997)

SEASON	CAPS
1990-91	6
1991-92	7
1992-93	8
1993-94	7
1994-95	8
1995-96	4
1996-97	5
Total	45

STAR QUOTE

'I am playing for the best side in the League, but there's still more to be done.'

Shrugging off the disappointment of rejection by Leeds United, Denis Irwin fought back to claim a bagful of honours with Manchester United and a successful international career. This refusal to accept failure is the very essence of a man whose faultless displays at full-back – on either side of the defence – have won him the respect of the critical Old Trafford audience.

Irwin arrived at Elland Road from his native Cork as a 16-year-old apprentice and looked set for a long run in the first team after making his debut two years later. But, after around 70 games, he lost his place and was offloaded to Oldham on a free transfer at the end of the 1985-86 season. This was to prove a minor setback, as Irwin caught the eye time and again with his forward forays and ultra-tight defending.

Considered the best right-back outside the First Division, the Irishman starred as Latics reached the FA Cup semi-final against the Reds in 1990, only giving way after a replay and extra-time. Alex Ferguson, though, had seen enough and splashed out £625,000 to bring him back into the top flight.

His performance against United's formidable strikeforce had, said his new boss, 'underlined his potential' and taken him from a shortlist candidate to United player. Jack Charlton, the Republic of Ireland boss, was impressed, too, and gave Denis his first taste of full international football after he'd played just two games in a red shirt.

Descriptions of the defensive capabilities of 1990s United usually highlighted the contributions of Pallister and Schmeichel, but Irwin would make his mark in his own way. An unflappable temperament – 'I'm not the worrying sort,' he smiles – together with a genuine two-footed capability make him a valuable if relatively unsung contributor to the team effort.

Irwin was soon United's Mr Dependable and one of the first players selected, a fine repertoire of dead-ball skills – 'the best at the club', according to Peter Schmeichel – adding to his defensive soundness. Every major honour that fell the club's

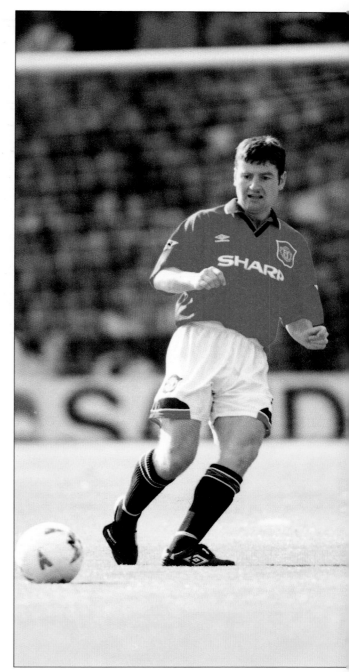

way in the phenomenal run of the 1990s was shared by Irwin, his name ever-present during the first Double season of 1993-94. A World Cup Finals appearance with the Republic of Ireland in America his proudest moment, Denis Irwin remained a valuable squad member at the close of the 1996-97 season.

Roy Keane

PERSONAL FILE

Born: 10 August 1971
Birthplace: Cork
Height: 5' 10"
Weight: 12st 10lb

LEAGUE RECORD

FROM-TO	CLUB	APPS	GOALS
1990-93	Nott'm Forest	114	22
1993-97	Manchester Utd	112	15
Total		226	37

MANCHESTER UNITED LEAGUE DEBUT

15 August 1993 v Norwich City

EIRE DEBUT

22 May 1991 v Chile

EIRE HONOURS (TO 31 MAY 1997)

SEASON	CAPS
1990-91	1
1991-92	6
1992-93	9
1993-94	10
1994-95	2
1995-96	2
1996-97	5
Total	35

STAR QUOTE

'I believe in passion and commitment: I set myself high standards and I push myself hard.'

A hidden talent plucked from obscurity by the legendary Brian Clough, Roy Keane has taken over the mantle of Bryan Robson and Paul Ince and is a cult hero to the Manchester United hordes.

Brought to England from Cobh Ramblers for a bargain £10,000 in 1990, Keane quickly made his mark at Nottingham Forest and was soon called up by the Republic of Ireland. However, Forest's relegation in 1993 made a move inevitable and Alex Ferguson paid £3.75 million, then an English record, for his services. An immediate hit, Keane's first season was an astonishing one, with only defeat in the League Cup Final preventing a domestic Treble.

An all-round player, who blends fine distribution and powerful running with a fierce, devil-may-care competitiveness, Keane is a throwback to the days of Dave Mackay.

His enthusiasm sometimes gets the better of him, as illustrated by his 1995 FA Cup semi-final sending-off for stamping on Crystal Palace's Gareth Southgate. Indeed, his poor disciplinary record is cause for concern with United battling on so many fronts in the 1990s, but Ferguson sees his buccaneering style as the perfect foil for the likes of Beckham and Giggs.

With two Doubles to his name and a World Cup Finals appearance in 1994, Keane has already scaled heights few players, especially those starting at Cobh Ramblers, can dream of. At the relatively young age of 26 in August 1997, he has the game to become part of United folklore if his tendency to hot-headedness matures into pure, cold-eyed aggression.

1967-1974

Brian Kidd

DID YOU KNOW?
Brian Kidd made 13 appearances in red in Manchester derbies, as opposed to six in the blue shirt of City.

Currently assistant manager at Old Trafford, Brian Kidd burst onto the first-team scene as a player in 1967-68, capping his first season with a call-up to the European Cup-winning side in place of the injured Denis Law. Playing in the week of his 19th birthday, he killed off the game with United's third goal, the second to be scored in extra time.

He was unfortunate enough to play most of his United football in the post-Busby era, but his all-round forward skills shone through to earn two England caps under Alf Ramsey. He'd score in his second game, a World Cup warm-up in Ecuador in which he substituted for City's Francis Lee, but he had already been overlooked for the final 22-man squad and this was too late to change matters.

On United's relegation in 1974, he retained his top-flight status by moving south to Arsenal for a two-year spell, playing alongside first Radford and then Stapleton, in which he significantly improved his goals-to-games ratio.

Next came a surprise return to Manchester, this time in City's colours. Everton signed him in 1979, giving him the distinction of having played in all three major English derbies – United v City (for both sides), Arsenal v Spurs and Liverpool v Everton. Yet another return to Greater Manchester with Bolton was followed by a spell in America, and – on

hanging up his boots – a brief time as Preston's manager.

His recruitment to the United coaching staff under Alex Ferguson coincided with the club's greatest success since his playing days, and it seems likely that Kidd will be the appointed successor if and when Fergie retires at the end of his current contract.

Denis Law

PERSONAL FILE

Born: 24 February 1940
Birthplace: Aberdeen
Height: 5' 9"
Weight: 10st 5lb

LEAGUE RECORD

FROM-TO	CLUB	APPS	GOALS
1956-60	Huddersfield T	81	16
1960-61	Manchester C	44	21
1961-62	Torino	N/K	N/K
1962-73	Manchester Utd	309	171
1973-74	Manchester C	24	9
Total		458	217

MANCHESTER UNITED LEAGUE DEBUT

18 August 1962 v West Bromwich Albion

SCOTLAND DEBUT

18 October 1958 v Wales

SCOTLAND HONOURS

SEASON	CAPS
1958-59	4
1959-60	5
1960-61	2
1961-62	3
1962-63	7
1963-64	4
1964-65	7
1965-66	3
1966-67	3
1967-68	1
1968-69	3
1969-70	—
1970-71	—
1971-72	7
1972-73	—
1973-74	6
Total	55

DID YOU KNOW?

'Crippled Law the hero with two goals' read the headline as United clinched the 1965 title with a 3-1 win against Arsenal.

Aberdeen-born Denis Law will be forever associated with the city of Manchester, after three spells with its two teams. Yet he was not only one of his country's international greats, recalled to the squad in his mid-thirties, but also one of the first British players to enjoy a spell in Italy, and his rare talents twice attracted British record transfer fees.

A first-team player at 16 at Huddersfield, the Scot arrived at Old Trafford via Manchester City, and Torino. Matt Busby invested £115,000 in his goalscoring knack, and 23 goals in 38 games and a Cup Final strike in the win over Leicester was quite a return in his first season. Little wonder he was the highest-paid player in Britain, and European Footballer of the Year in 1964.

Law was an Old Trafford fixture for the glory years, though he missed the European Cup Final through injury. His place in a forward line with Charlton, Herd and Best made him one of 1960s football's legends, his goals helping United to League titles in 1965 and 1967: the former season saw him set a Fairs (now UEFA) Cup record of nine goals with a team that didn't even get to the Final.

A much-loved figure at Old Trafford, Law's trademark one-armed goal salute became as much a part of United legend as his flapping shirt and trademark 'salmon' leap: not for nothing was he nicknamed 'the King'. His first five seasons with United before injury dug deeply saw him harvest 160 goals from 222 matches in all competitions – a phenomenal strike rate in anyone's language.

Law's last season in League football was at

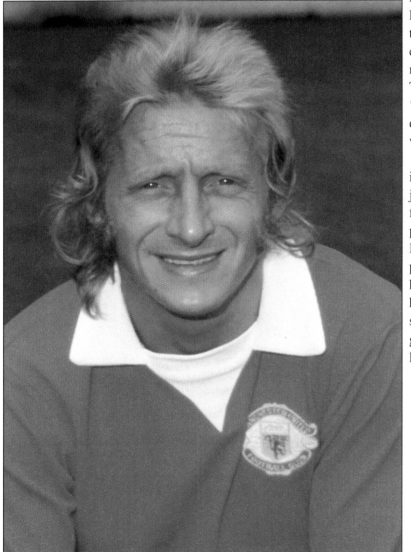

Manchester City, after Tommy Docherty turned to younger talents, and his backheeled goal consigned his former team-mates to a spell in Division Two – their first for 36 years. 'I have seldom been so depressed as I was that weekend,' he later revealed.

His anticipation, predatory instinct and spring-heeled jumping made Law an exciting figure to watch, though his personality could be volatile. Injury caused increasing problems, especially in his knee, but his whole-heartedness wouldn't let him shirk on workrate, and many goals came from chasing lost causes.

At Manchester City, Denis once scored six goals in a game, only to have them washed out when the rain caused its abandonment.

51

Brian McClair

PERSONAL FILE

Born: 8 December 1963
Birthplace: Airdrie
Height: 5' 10"
Weight: 12st 12lb

LEAGUE RECORD

FROM-TO	CLUB	APPS	GOALS
1980-81	Aston Villa	—	—
1981-83	Motherwell	39	15
1983-87	Celtic	145	99
1987-97	Manchester Utd	342	88
Total		526	202

MANCHESTER UNITED LEAGUE DEBUT

15 August 1987 v Southampton

SCOTLAND DEBUT

12 November 1986 v Luxembourg

SCOTLAND HONOURS

SEASON	CAPS
1986-87	4
1987-88	3
1988-89	5
1989-90	2
1990-91	3
1991-92	9
1992-93	4
Total	30

STAR QUOTE

'I want to stay with United until the end of my playing career.'

Mr Versatility, or Brian McClair as he is known outside Old Trafford, clocked up his tenth year at Manchester United in the summer of 1997 and for loyalty and consistency has few peers. Written off at the beginning of each season, he continually confounds his critics and has been given a new contract for 1997-98.

When Airdrie-born McClair, who was an apprentice with Aston Villa for a year before returning north of the border, arrived at the club for £850,000 in July 1987, he was already an accomplished striker and Scotland's Player of the Year, having won League and Cup honours in a four-year stay at Celtic.

A strong, skilful 23-year-old, McClair's deadly finishing proved equally effective in the First Division, his total of 24 goals in his debut season being the first to top 20 since George Best registered 28 in 1968.

Alex Ferguson, though, saw talents in his fellow Scot that others had overlooked and, as his career progressed, McClair took on a role just behind Mark Hughes, his perceptive passing and unselfish running off the ball adding to United's cutting edge. Success followed, and the Scotland international has a trophy cabinet second to none, every domestic honour his as well as a European Cup Winners' Cup medal. Branded the 'model professional' by his manager, McClair's goal won the 1992 League Cup and he also scored in the 1994 FA Cup Final.

Though his role has become an increasingly occasional one, McClair's adaptability is seen as a key part of United's success as he approaches his 34th birthday. His contribution was recognised in a testimonial against Celtic in 1997.

Paul McGrath

PERSONAL FILE

Born: 4 December 1959
Birthplace: Ealing
Height: 6' 2"
Weight: 14st 0lb

LEAGUE RECORD

FROM-TO	CLUB	APPS	GOALS
1982-89	Manchester Utd	163	12
1989-96	Aston Villa	253	9
1996-97	Derby Co	24	—
Total		440	21

MANCHESTER UNITED LEAGUE DEBUT

13 November 1982 v Tottenham Hotspur

EIRE DEBUT

5 February 1985 v Italy

EIRE HONOURS (TO 31 MAY 1997)

SEASON	CAPS
1984-85	5
1985-86	5
1986-87	8
1987-88	7
1988-89	6
1989-90	10
1990-91	6
1991-92	8
1992-93	6
1993-94	8
1994-95	7
1995-96	6
1996-97	1
Total	83

STAR QUOTE

'Never did I go on the pitch the worse for wear... I gave my all for United.'

'Oh, ah, Paul McGrath' ran the Stretford End's favourite song – and the centre-back that inspired it earned a lasting place in United fans' affections, if occasionally providing his managers with a headache or two thanks to a self-confessed hellraising lifestyle.

Born in England but of Irish parentage, McGrath re-crossed the Irish Sea at the end of April 1982, costing United £30,000. The former St Patrick's Athletic youngster wouldn't make his debut until the following November, though, with Moran, McQueen and Buchan already contesting the two central defensive berths. It proved a one-off appearance, but once he forced his way back in March 1983, McGrath played out the rest of a successful campaign.

Two more part seasons followed as he grappled with injuries, before he became a first-team regular in 1985-86 – the same year he pushed Gary Lineker close for the PFA Player of the Year award. Yet his off-pitch unpredictability didn't endear him to Alex Ferguson, and, once Gary Pallister came on the market, Paul was on his way.

A transfer to Aston Villa, where he'd play again under former manager Ron Atkinson, proved he still had it in him to compete for honours, though his suspect knees were always a cause for concern. Even so, he helped Villa to the League (Coca-Cola) Cup in both 1994 and 1996 to prove the medics wrong.

McGrath's knees are worthy of an article in themselves. His first serious problem came in 1982 with a twisted knee, which necessitated a cartilage operation. Then in 1987 he had another op, this time on the right knee, but after an injury sustained in the following year's European Championships he was told his career would last no longer than another three months. The right knee has had its meniscus or natural shock absorber removed which may lead to future problems.

He'd been a regular in the Eire international side since 1986, flourishing under Jack Charlton and taking his total caps to 83 by the summer of 1997. The previous year he moved from Villa to newly-promoted Derby, where he helped them retain their Premiership status before receiving a free transfer. Now a happy family man, but well into the veteran stage, his next move was awaited with interest.

1971-1982

Sammy McIlroy

STAR QUOTE

'People said the 1974 team was the worst United side for years – we hadn't shown the form people expected.'

Belfast, famous for giving Manchester United George Best, also supplied Sammy McIlroy, whose effective, enthusiastic style could not be compared to his famous compatriot, but earned him 88 Northern Ireland caps to Best's 37, his first as a raw 17-year-old in 1972.

McIlroy faced the fiercest of debuts in the 1971 Manchester derby at Maine Road, just two years after becoming an apprentice. A slim, darting midfield player, McIlroy scored the opening goal as the sides fought out a 3-3 draw. But, held back by his inexperience and injuries suffered in a car accident, the young Irishman had to wait until the 1973-74 season before establishing his place in Tommy Docherty's side alongside the equally skilful Lou Macari.

McIlroy's career reached its lowest ebb with relegation in 1974, but his all-action, 90-minute style, which regularly carried him into goalscoring positions, was a major factor as United bounced straight back as Champions. It seems something of an injustice that he had just one FA Cup winner's medal (1977) to show for three trips to Wembley in the 1970s.

Sammy McIlroy clocked up 390 appearances for the club, scoring 70 goals, before signing for Stoke in 1982. He served his new side with equal distinction before returning to Manchester with City.

McIlroy, who finished his playing career at Preston North End, will be remembered as one of Docherty's exciting young entertainers who restored United's pride. The most capped Northern Ireland player in Manchester United's history, McIlroy's services to professional football have been recognised by an MBE, and his managerial skills were apparent when he led Macclesfield Town into the Football League in 1997.

Gordon McQueen

PERSONAL FILE

Born: 26 June 1952
Birthplace: Kilbirnie
Height: 6' 4"
Weight: 13st 6lb

LEAGUE RECORD

FROM-TO	CLUB	APPS	GOALS
1970-72	St Mirren	57	5
1972-78	Leeds Utd	140	15
1978-85	Manchester Utd	184	20
Total		381	40

MANCHESTER UNITED LEAGUE DEBUT

25 February 1978 v Liverpool

SCOTLAND DEBUT

2 June 1974 v Belgium

SCOTLAND HONOURS

SEASON	CAPS
1973-74	1
1974-75	7
1975-76	1
1976-77	5
1977-78	6
1978-79	6
1979-80	3
1980-81	1
Total	30

STAR QUOTE

'While United have been more successful recently, the atmosphere in my day was that bit more electric.'

Manchester United, who were later to enjoy the best years of unexpected Leeds United cast-offs Denis Irwin and Eric Cantona, had earlier raided Elland Road for Gordon McQueen. The Scot became a towering presence in their defence for eight seasons, after signing in February 1978 for just short of £500,000.

McQueen, a huge but agile centre-half with wonderfully quick feet for a man of six foot four, had joined Leeds from St Mirren six years previously. An established international, he helped bring the Championship to Yorkshire in 1974 and his capture by Dave Sexton was seen as a coup, especially as Leeds had also allowed fellow Scotland star Joe Jordan to join United a few weeks earlier.

Tough and sometimes uncompromising in the tackle, McQueen went on to play 228 times for United in all competitions, his 26 goals a marvellous bonus and largely the result of unstoppable headers from corners and free-kicks. Prone to injury through his sheer size, he was regularly on the treatment table until serious damage sustained in the early part of 1984 effectively brought his playing career to a halt.

Gordon's enthusiasm for the game was legendary: his father played League football for now-defunct Accrington Stanley, while shortly after arriving at Leeds United he was to be seen on Sunday mornings watching his local amateur teams in Roundhay Park.

Like his contemporaries of the late 1970s and early 1980s, McQueen's medal collection bears no relation to his ability, the 1983 FA Cup win over Brighton his sole success from three visits to Wembley. Another disappointment was his failure to play in the World Cup Finals, for which Scotland qualified three times running from 1974. McQueen joined Seiko of Hong Kong as player-coach in 1985, before returning to undertake numerous coaching positions. He ended the 1996-97 season assisting Bryan Robson at Middlesbrough.

Kevin Moran

PERSONAL FILE

Born: 29 April 1956
Birthplace: Dublin
Height: 5' 11"
Weight: 12st 9lb

LEAGUE RECORD

FROM-TO	CLUB	APPS	GOALS
1978-88	Manchester Utd	231	21
1988-90	Sporting Gijon	n/k	n/k
1990-94	Blackburn R	147	10
Total		378	31

MANCHESTER UNITED LEAGUE DEBUT

30 April 1979 v Southampton

EIRE DEBUT

30 April 1980 v Switzerland

EIRE HONOURS

SEASON	CAPS
1979-80	2
1980-81	8
1981-82	2
1982-83	1
1983-84	4
1984-85	1
1985-86	3
1986-87	8
1987-88	10
1988-89	6
1989-90	10
1990-91	6
1991-92	2
1992-93	4
1993-94	4
Total	71

DID YOU KNOW?

When policeman Peter Willis consigned Kevin to the Cup Final sidelines, it was the first dismissal in 116 matches in 113 years.

Kevin Moran's hard-man reputation, earned more by his unstinting bravery than any nasty streak, seemed on the face of it to be justified when, in 1985, he became the first player ever to be sent off in an FA Cup Final at Wembley.

Moran, a defender of the old school who refused to give anything less than 100 per cent every time he took the field, mistimed a challenge on Everton's Peter Reid and, despite protests from both sides, was sent back down the tunnel.

And the drama wasn't over, for he was initially refused a winner's medal after ten-man United's extra-time victory. However, common sense prevailed and the unlucky Irishman received his memento after an appeal.

The Dubliner, who had arrived from Irish college football in 1978, was at this time an automatic choice at the heart of the United defence and had been since the 1980-81 season, forming a formidable rearguard with Gordon McQueen until the Scot's surrender to injury. Indeed, Moran himself was to spend many unwanted weeks on the sidelines, his determination to throw everything at every game coming at a high price.

Unlike the stable Pallister-Bruce combination of recent years, Kevin would see many different faces slot in beside him at the centre of the United back four. His first pairing had been with Martin Buchan before McQueen's arrival: then Scotsman Graeme Hogg, Irishman Paul McGrath and Billy Garton cropped up beside him.

When Moran departed for Sporting Gijon in August 1988, he had played 17 short of 300 games for United and been part of two FA Cup-winning teams.

Back in England to join Blackburn in 1990, he retired the season before they won the Premier

League Championship in 1995, having been in the Republic of Ireland's 1994 World Cup Finals squad aged 38.

One of his central defensive partners had been David May, who would make the return journey from Ewood Park to Old Trafford – though not with a Spanish stop-off – just as he retired. If May could enjoy as long and fruitful a career as the Irishman, he would indeed have done well.

1982- 1985

Arnold Muhren

PERSONAL FILE

Born: 2 June 1951
Birthplace: Volendam, Holland
Height: 5' 9"
Weight: 10st 12lb

LEAGUE RECORD

FROM-TO	CLUB	APPS	GOALS
1978-82	Ipswich T	161	21
1982-85	Manchester Utd	70	13
Total		231	34

MANCHESTER UNITED LEAGUE DEBUT

28 August 1982 v Birmingham City

HOLLAND HONOURS

n/k

DID YOU KNOW?

In his first spell at Ajax, Arnold was a substitute in the 1972 and 1973 European Cup Finals, but didn't get on in either game.

When Arnold Muhren departed for his native Holland and former club Ajax in 1985 at the age of 34, few could have predicted the glories that still lay ahead for the supremely talented midfield playmaker with the Continental touch.

Muhren had begun his career with the Amsterdam giants and was in the squad that won two European Cups, but was far from a household name when he arrived at Ipswich in 1978.

However, in more than 200 games at Portman Road, he treated the East Anglian fans to his full, dazzling repertoire, his artist's brush of a left foot scoring spectacular goals and creating hosts of others. It was this brilliance that persuaded Ron Atkinson to take him north when his contract expired in 1982.

In just 92 games, Muhren enraptured Old Trafford with his elegant displays, scoring 18 goals and twice going to Wembley, losing the League Cup to Liverpool and beating Brighton two months later to lift the 1983 FA Cup.

The following season, Muhren helped United into a challenging position for the title until his campaign was cut short by injury. He would never enjoy a regular place again and returned to his native Holland with barely a whisper.

It was significant that United's Championship challenge faded as their playmaker sat on the sidelines. He was replaced by Norman Whiteside, who dropped back into midfield to accommodate up and coming striker Mark Hughes. The summer signing of Gordon Strachan blocked further progress.

But age was obviously no barrier to Ajax, and Muhren was to produce some of his finest football as a veteran. Indeed, as a 37-year-old, the master craftsman could be seen at work in Holland's midfield as they won the 1988 European Championships in West Germany, with many an appreciative United fan willing them on.

1993-1997

Gary Neville

STAR QUOTE

'If you need motivating to play for Manchester United, then you shouldn't be at the club.'

One of several products of Manchester United's prolific 1992 Youth Cup-winning side, Gary Neville is – at just 22 – an established member of the England set-up. Yet, such is the clamour for places at Old Trafford, that for a spell in the 1995-96 season he was kept on the sidelines by his younger brother Philip, also a full international.

Gary, an orthodox right-back, can also operate in the centre of defence and many see his future in this position despite his relative lack of height. He made his first appearance for the Reds as a substitute against Torpedo Moscow in the UEFA Cup in September 1992, aged just 17. His first full League game came against Coventry in the final Premiership match of 1993-94, and he has become more or less a permanent fixture since then. Calm and composed under pressure, Neville's distribution from the back is first class and his crossing superb, if slightly inconsistent. A solid header of the ball, Gary's long throw has become a valued weapon in the United arsenal.

The elder Neville's international career was also quick to materialise. A youth and Under-18 international, he by-passed the Under-21 team to 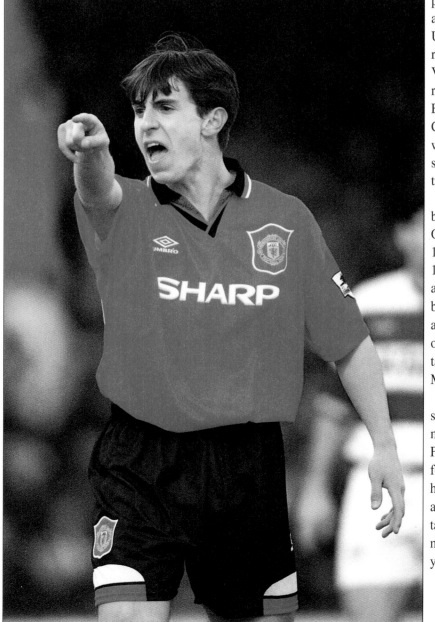 play for the senior side against Japan in the 1995 Umbro Cup, and was a regular under Terry Venables as England reached the semi-finals of Euro '96, his United Championship and FA Cup winner's medals already safely in the family trophy cabinet.

Phil and Gary were both very much part of the Old Trafford set-up in 1996-97. Phil notched up 19 Premiership appearances, while his brother registered 31. Gary also won the race to be first on the scoresheet when on target against Middlesbrough in May.

Another Championship season later, Neville, like most of Fergie's Fledglings, has the footballing world before him. The European Cup and World Cup are obvious targets in 1998 for this modest, unassuming young professional.

Jimmy Nicholl

PERSONAL FILE

Born: 28 February 1956
Birthplace: Hamilton, Canada
Height: 5' 10"
Weight: 11st 10lb

LEAGUE RECORD

FROM-TO	CLUB	APPS	GOALS
1974-81	Manchester Utd	197	3
1981-82	Sunderland (loan)	3	—
1982	Toronto Blizzard	16	3
1982-83	Sunderland	29	—
1983-84	Toronto Blizzard	49	8
1983-84	Rangers	17	—
1984-86	West Brom	56	—
1986-89	Rangers	65	—
1989-90	Dunfermline Ath	24	—
1990-95	Raith R	128	7
Total		584	21

MANCHESTER UNITED LEAGUE DEBUT

5 April 1975 v Southampton

NORTHERN IRELAND DEBUT

3 March 1976 v Israel

NORTHERN IRELAND HONOURS

SEASON	CAPS
1975-76	2
1976-77	6
1977-78	6
1978-79	9
1979-80	9
1980-81	6
1981-82	10
1982-83	8
1983-84	5
1984-85	5
1985-86	7
Total	73

DID YOU KNOW?

Jimmy experienced two of the most intense atmospheres football can offer in the Manchester and Glasgow derbies.

A popular right-back with Manchester United and Northern Ireland, Jimmy Nicholl was, in fact, born in Canada though his parents moved to Belfast when he was a child. Like many youngsters from that area, Nicholl adored United and he joined as an apprentice straight from school.

Offered professional terms in 1974, Nicholl waited a year for his debut against Southampton and grabbed his chance when first-team regular Alex Forsyth was injured in the 1976-77 season. Composure on the ball and tight marshalling skills, backed by pace and a crunching tackle were contributing factors that kept him employed for five seasons.

Nicholl's consistency had also attracted Northern Ireland, who went on to cap their adopted son 41 times as a United player. An FA Cup winner's medal to the good, Nicholl had every reason to be pleased.

However, things quickly turned sour with the arrival of Ron Atkinson in summer 1981. Atkinson drafted in John Gidman from Everton, and Nicholl's career at Old Trafford was over.

He was loaned to Sunderland before a move to Toronto Blizzard, based in the land of his birth, in 1982. Later spells with Glasgow Rangers proved fruitful for Nicholl, who won a Championship and a Cup: he also took his total of international caps to 73, including two World Cup Finals.

His playing days now numbered, Nicholl quickly found success as a manager, guiding Raith Rovers to the Scottish First Division Championship and a momentous Cup Final victory over Celtic. However, his first job in England proved disastrous when he was sacked by Second Division Millwall early in 1997. He was reinstalled at Raith in time for the new season.

Gary Pallister

PERSONAL FILE

Born: 30 June 1965
Birthplace: Ramsgate
Height: 6' 4"
Weight: 14st 13lb

LEAGUE RECORD

FROM-TO	CLUB	APPS	GOALS
1984-89	Middlesbrough	156	5
1985	Darlington (loan)	7	—
1989-97	Manchester Utd	284	12
Total		447	17

MANCHESTER UNITED LEAGUE DEBUT

30 August 1989 v Norwich City

ENGLAND DEBUT

27 April 1988 v Hungary

ENGLAND HONOURS (TO 31 MAY 1997)

SEASON	CAPS
1987-88	1
1988-89	1
1989-90	—
1990-91	2
1991-92	1
1992-93	4
1993-94	4
1994-95	5
1995-96	2
1996-97	2
Total	22

STAR QUOTE

Gary might not have been signed had Alex Ferguson succeeded in a 1989 bid for Fiorentina's Glenn Hysen. Liverpool got Glenn, United the better of the deal.

Gary Pallister's central defensive partnership with Steve Bruce is arguably the most successful rearguard link forged in decades, with eight major trophies, including two Doubles, arriving at Old Trafford in five years during the early 1990s.

But this level of achievement looked a million miles away back in 1989, when the lanky Pallister arrived from Middlesbrough for £2.3 million, a British record at the time. Despite his calm, measured appearance, he looked hesitant under pressure and the media was quickly doubting the wisdom of the move. How wrong time proved them to be.

Pallister's confidence grew as his partnership with Bruce developed, the latter's experience a crucial factor. Tremendously powerful in the air – as Liverpool found to their cost when he converted two corners at Anfield in April 1997 – and surprisingly swift for a six-foot-four-inch giant, Pallister was named PFA Player of the Year in 1992 and rejuvenated an England career which had begun at Boro. However, he suffered a rare setback to his ambitions when injury ruled him out of Terry Venables' squad for the 1996 European Championships, a disappointment moderated by his club side's second domestic Double.

The Ramsgate-born defender, who began his playing days with Billingham Town, almost joined Darlington when his Middlesbrough career took a wobble in 1985. But his determination to succeed at the highest level saw him through. 'I've done YTS schemes and worked in the docks,' he said, 'so I know what the alternative to football is.'

Deprived of his usual defensive partner when Steve Bruce moved to Birmingham in the summer of 1996, Gary understandably found teething troubles in his new partnership with David May, yet still picked up his fourth Championship medal in 1996-97. Pallister is well on his way to 400 United appearances in all competitions, and that £2.3 million continues to look money well spent.

'Championships are won over a
season – it's a cliché, like the marathon
analogy, but it's true.'

Bryan Robson

PERSONAL FILE

Born: 11 January 1957
Birthplace: Chester-le-Street
Height: 5' 9"
Weight: 12st 5lb

LEAGUE RECORD

FROM-TO	CLUB	APPS	GOALS
1974-81	West Brom	197	39
1981-94	Manchester Utd	345	74
1994-97	Middlesbrough	25	1
Total		567	114

MANCHESTER UNITED LEAGUE DEBUT

10 October 1981 v Manchester City

ENGLAND DEBUT

6 February 1980 v Eire

ENGLAND HONOURS

SEASON	CAPS
1979-80	2
1980-81	10
1981-82	11
1982-83	4
1983-84	9
1984-85	11
1985-86	6
1986-87	6
1987-88	10
1988-89	10
1989-90	8
1990-91	2
1991-92	1
Total	90

STAR QUOTE

'I haven't found management difficult at all. The only thing I've found difficult is taking relegation.'

Among the most courageous of players ever to wear the red of Manchester United, Bryan Robson developed from an unvarnished 15-year-old talent at West Bromwich Albion into a world-class midfielder admired the world over. He led his club and country by example, playing 432 games for United and 90 for England, and would have topped a century of caps but for injury. When he left to become Middlesbrough player-manager in 1994, fittingly on the back of the club's first Double, he had been an inspiration for 13 years.

Robson, born in Chester-le-Street, trialled with several clubs including Newcastle before arriving at the Hawthorns in September 1972. In 1975, he made his first-team breakthrough, but his progress was halted by three broken legs in a year. Showing the determination that was to become his trademark, Robson battled his way back, as he was forced to on many subsequent occasions.

West Brom manager Ron Atkinson moved to Old Trafford in 1981 and, in the most telling move during his reign, brought 24-year-old Robson to the club in a £2 million double deal involving Remi Moses. Soon appointed captain, Robson was a revelation. Stamina, aggression, fearless tackling, shrewd distribution, powerful heading and a priceless goalscorer's intuition all combined to make him unique.

Robson scored 97 goals for United and 26 for England, including a hat-trick and a 27-second effort against France in the 1982 World Cup Finals. Led out of the 1986 tournament with a dislocated shoulder, he was back in action for a third attempt four years later. With a collection of Championship, Cup and European medals, the small boy from the north-east who emerged as his country's lionheart can look back on a glittering career with pride.

His career as Boro player-manager started splendidly as they won promotion to the top flight, backed by a big budget. Once there, Robson bought the best in Juninho and Ravanelli, but though his team reached both domestic Cup Finals in 1996-97 they slid to relegation as United were claiming their fourth Premiership title. Having hung up his boots, the former Captain Marvel was finding it difficult to motivate his men from an off-field position.

'I was fortunate enough to play under Bryan at international level, and he was a fabulous skipper and a fabulous player.'
TONY ADAMS

Peter Schmeichel

PERSONAL FILE

Born: 18 November 1963
Birthplace: Gladsaxe, Denmark
Height: 6' 4"
Weight: 15st 13lb

LEAGUE RECORD

FROM-TO	CLUB	APPS	GOALS
1984-86	Hvidovre	88	6
1987-91	Brondby	119	2
1991-97	Manchester Utd	216	—
Total		423	8

MANCHESTER UNITED LEAGUE DEBUT

17 August 1991 v Notts County

DENMARK HONOURS

Had been capped 87 times by his country by the start of the 1996-97 season

STAR QUOTE

'Schmeichel is the best in the world.'
ALEX FERGUSON

When the imposing Peter Schmeichel arrived at Manchester United from Danish Champions Brondby in August 1991, he was his country's Player of the Year for the second time and an established international. On that basis alone, his £550,000 pricetag looked small beer and subsequent events mark the deal as one of the bargains of the century.

Schmeichel, a towering six foot four and 16 stones, was soon dominating his area and marshalling his defenders, keeping 17 clean sheets as runners-up United returned the best defensive record in the League in 1991-92.

A 1-0 League Cup Final victory over Nottingham Forest gave the Great Dane the first of many domestic honours, but his reputation was to take a huge boost in the summer when unfancied late entrants Denmark lifted the European Championship with a 2-0 victory over Germany in Sweden, Schmeichel's acrobatics in the semi-final penalty shoot-out with Holland a talking point for weeks.

Schmeichel's consistency provided the foundation of United's phenomenal success in the 1990s as his high standards rubbed off on all around him. Time and again in the 1995-96 Double campaign, his saves proved the difference between victory and defeat, with just 29 goals conceded in 36 League games and only nine at fortress Old Trafford. United's best ever keeper? Unquestionably. One of the best in the world? Definitely.

Again in 1996-97 he showed his consistency by missing just two League games during the season. The goals against column, however, was less impressive than before thanks to those two memorable early-season defeats against Newcastle (0-5) and Southampton (3-6).

Schmeichel's value as an attacker is also worth documenting. The sight of him launching a quick throw-out beyond the halfway line is accepted as normal and who can forget him rising in Rotor Volgograd's penalty area to head a late equaliser in a 1995-96 UEFA Cup tie?

With almost 300 appearances to his name, the charismatic Dane has repaid his fee a thousand times already.

'He's so big,
    so difficult to get the ball past.'
                    DALIAN ATKINSON

Paul Scholes

PERSONAL FILE

Born: 16 November 1974
Birthplace: Salford
Height: 5' 7"
Weight: 11st 0lb

LEAGUE RECORD

FROM-TO	CLUB	APPS	GOALS
1993-97	Manchester Utd	68	19

MANCHESTER UNITED LEAGUE DEBUT

24 September 1994 v Ipswich Town

ENGLAND DEBUT

24 May 1997 v South Africa

ENGLAND HONOURS (TO 31 MAY 1997)

SEASON	CAPS
1996-97	1
Total	1

STAR QUOTE

'Scholesey is a star in the making – he's red hot in training, has a cracking shot and a real eye for goal.'
STEVE BRUCE

When Paul Scholes, making his full England debut against South Africa as a second-half replacement for Teddy Sheringham at Old Trafford in May 1997, set up the winning goal for Ian Wright, the feat was all the more remarkable because the 22-year-old Salford-born redhead was still unable to command a first-team place at Manchester United.

Scholes, an England Youth international, burst onto the scene in the 1994-95 season with two goals on his debut in a Coca-Cola Cup tie. Alex Ferguson, denied the services of the banned Eric Cantona, used Scholes mainly as a substitute and the stocky powerhouse showed an uncanny awareness for one so young, also netting on his Premiership bow at Ipswich. He finished the season with seven goals from just ten full starts and 15 from the bench.

As United clinched the Double for the second time the following season, Scholes proved an invaluable squad member, his 13 goals in all competitions testament to his finisher's instinct. His consistency at finding the target seemed sure to guarantee him a run in the side, but with Andy Cole and Ole Gunnar Solskjaer the first choices in 1996-97, his opportunities were surprisingly infrequent.

It is impossible to see Scholes being content with a bit-part role forever, even within a squad as imposing and successful as United's. An ambitious lad, Scholes would be a first choice at every other club in the country and a red-hot property in the transfer market. Whatever the outcome, Scholes, once dubbed 'United's Kenny Dalglish' by his manager, has a big future in football.

And that future may well have brightened considerably with the departure of Eric Cantona. Having been groomed to take the Frenchman's role, Scholes could not yet be expected to provide the leadership qualities the inspirational Frenchman had gathered through a lengthy career: these would come from Teddy Sheringham. He would undoubtedly have the chance to improve on the 17 starts, eight substitute appearances and four goals he registered in 1996-97.

Lee Sharpe

PERSONAL FILE

Born: 27 May 1971
Birthplace: Halesowen
Height: 6' 0"
Weight: 12st 6lb

LEAGUE RECORD

FROM-TO	CLUB	APPS	GOALS
1988	Torquay Utd	14	3
1988-96	Manchester Utd	193	21
1996-97	Leeds Utd	26	4
Total		233	28

MANCHESTER UNITED LEAGUE DEBUT

24 September 1988 v West Ham United

ENGLAND DEBUT

27 March 1991 v Eire

ENGLAND HONOURS

SEASON	CAPS
1990-91	1
1991-92	—
1992-93	5
1993-94	2
Total	8

STAR QUOTE

'He is not a flatterer: he is a deliverer. He can produce killer crosses, and can finish too.'
ALEX FERGUSON

In a career hampered by illness and injury, Lee Sharpe packed in almost 200 League appearances before leaving for Leeds in the summer of 1996. In eight years, Sharpe accumulated more honours at club and international level than most would in a career, yet on his departure he was just 25.

Reports of Sharpe's promise were relayed to Manchester from Torquay, where he had made his League debut at just 16, and the club invested £185,000 for him in June 1988.

He played in 20 games in his first season and became England's youngest Under-21 cap. In 1989-90 Sharpe, who had been used mainly as a left-back, took up his natural position on the wing and was soon demonstrating his superb ball control, often at top pace.

His wicked left-foot crosses were causing havoc in opposing defences, but disaster struck as injury forced him out of the second half of the season. This was the first of many such interruptions, but Sharpe bounced back every time and became the youngest player since Duncan Edwards to play for England's senior side in 1991, two months before his 20th birthday. He was also voted the PFA's Young Player of the Year.

Lee's Old Trafford career was stopped in its tracks twice: once by a bad dose of viral meningitis in 1992, but earlier than that by Alex Ferguson's decision to play him at left wing-back. He liked nothing better than to attack and, after scoring, initiate the famous 'Shape Shuffle' which seemed to get him maximum publicity.

As United went on to dominate the Premiership from its inception in 1992-93, Sharpe's appearances were increasingly restricted, his seasonal totals being 27, 26, 26 and 21 respectively. Perhaps too similar in style to Ryan Giggs, Sharpe made way for the likes of summer inports Karel Poborsky and Jordi Cruyff and his England career also appeared over. But, if he can regain the form that marked him such a rare talent, he has time to re-establish himself among England's élite.

Ole Gunnar Solskjaer

PERSONAL FILE

Born: 26 February 1973
Birthplace: Kristiansund, Norway
Height: 5' 10"
Weight: 11st 10lb

LEAGUE RECORD

FROM-TO	CLUB	APPS	GOALS
1995	Molde	26	20
1996-97	Manchester Utd	32	17
Total		58	37

MANCHESTER UNITED LEAGUE DEBUT

26 August 1996 v Blackburn Rovers

NORWAY HONOURS

Had been capped five times by his country by the start of the 1996-97 season

DID YOU KNOW?
Ole could have joined Molde from his local club in 1993, but stayed on two years until he felt ready for the top flight.

O le Gunnar Solskjaer was handed the unenviable task of appeasing United fans disillusioned by the non-arrival at the club of Alan Shearer, who chose Newcastle instead in a record £15 million transfer in the 1995-96 close season.

Totally unheard of outside his native Norway, the 23-year-old Solskjaer arrived at Old Trafford in a £1.5 million deal from Molde and, at five foot ten and 11st 10lbs, would not have looked out of place in United's youth team. But, six minutes into his Premiership debut as a substitute against Blackburn, the young Scandinavian proved once again what an astute judge of talent manager Alex Ferguson is.

Of the new arrivals from Europe, which included the Czech Republic's Euro '96 star Karel Poborsky and the legendary Johann Cruyff's son Jordi, Solskjaer was the least heralded but proved easily the biggest asset.

Gifted with a sublime first touch, Solskjaer soon had the fans eating out of his hand as he found the target with comparative ease. Feeding hungrily off Eric Cantona in the early stages of the campaign and later forming a fine understanding with Andy Cole, the 'Baby Faced Assassin' ended his debut season with 17 League goals and a Championship winner's medal. Ferguson believes that Solskjaer 'is going to improve and improve', both physically and in other ways, in 1997-98.

Solskjaer, who appears to ghost into scoring positions, possesses a stinging shot in either foot and is deceptively strong on the ball, his shielding ability giving out faint echoes of an early Mark Hughes. If his progression matches his first-season endeavours, he will save the Reds a fortune in transfer fees.

Frank Stapleton

PERSONAL FILE

Born: 10 July 1956
Birthplace: Dublin
Height: 6' 0"
Weight: 13st 1lb

LEAGUE RECORD

FROM-TO	CLUB	APPS	GOALS
1973-81	Arsenal	225	75
1981-87	Manchester Utd	223	60
1987-88	Ajax	4	—
1988	Derby Co	10	1
1988-89	Le Havre	n/k	n/k
1989-91	Blackburn R	81	13
1991	Aldershot (loan)	1	—
1991	Huddersfield T	5	—
1991-94	Bradford C	68	2
1994-95	Brighton & HA	2	—
Total		619	151

MANCHESTER UNITED LEAGUE DEBUT

29 August 1981 v Coventry City

EIRE DEBUT

13 October 1976 v Turkey

EIRE HONOURS

SEASON	CAPS
1976-77	4
1977-78	3
1978-79	4
1979-80	5
1980-81	8
1981-82	3
1982-83	5
1983-84	6
1984-85	7
1985-86	6
1986-87	7
1987-88	8
1988-89	3
1989-90	2
Total	71

DID YOU KNOW?

Frank only scored twice in the League against United while with Arsenal, his first being his side's second in a final-match 2-3 defeat at Old Trafford in 1977.

Frank Stapleton's arrival at Manchester United from Arsenal in August 1981 cost the club approaching £1 million, and for a proven international striker with 75 top-flight goals to his credit few doubted the wisdom of the transaction. However, there were some red faces at Old Trafford, the Dublin-born hit-man having been rejected by United as a youngster before signing for the Gunners.

Stapleton, a strong, willing target man who gained as much pleasure from making goals for others as scoring them, was difficult to shake off the ball and often put his head in where it hurt. United fans had good reason to remember him, as he had scored in Arsenal's 3-2 win over the Reds in the 1979 FA Cup Final.

A regular choice for the Republic of Ireland, for whom he won 71 caps over 13 years, Stapleton went on to make 265 full appearances for United. Perhaps not as prolific in front of goal as he was at Highbury, his deft flicks and knock-downs were pure heaven for the likes of Norman Whiteside, Arnold Muhren and Bryan Robson. That said, Stapleton was often United's top scorer and banged in 78 goals in total, adding two more FA Cup winner's medals to his collection. His goal in the 1983 Final made him the first player to score for different clubs in two Wembley Finals.

Stapleton left United for Ajax in 1987 as a 31-year-old, but after a brief, unhappy stay made his way to Derby County. After a stint in France and two years at Blackburn, he entered a nomadic spell which saw him at several clubs, finally settling at Bradford as player-manager until the middle of 1994. He then moved to the States.

Bought initially to fill Joe Jordan's shoes as the Scot packed his bags for a lucrative spell in Serie A, Stapleton did rather more than that. In his six seasons at Old Trafford, he confirmed his position as one of the most complete strikers in the English game.

1966-1978

Alex Stepney

PERSONAL FILE

Born: 18 September 1942
Birthplace: Mitcham
Height: 6' 0"
Weight: 11st 9lb

LEAGUE RECORD

FROM-TO	CLUB	APPS	GOALS
1963-66	Millwall	137	—
1966	Chelsea	1	—
1966-78	Manchester Utd	433	2
1979-80	Dallas Tornado	54	—
Total		625	2

MANCHESTER UNITED LEAGUE DEBUT

17 September 1966 v Manchester City

ENGLAND DEBUT

22 May 1968 v Sweden

ENGLAND HONOURS

SEASON	CAPS
1967-68	1
Total	1

STAR QUOTE

'Like Alex Ferguson's side now we had a very good goalkeeper, which is important.'
BOBBY CHARLTON

A rare Cockney accent in the United dressing room, keeper Alex Stepney can claim League Championship and European Cup medals among his many honours in over a decade at the top – yet in international terms can count himself unlucky to have been understudying the England pair of Gordon Banks and Peter Bonetti.

Indeed, he came head to head with Bonetti for a brief while after crossing London from Millwall – his first professional club – to Chelsea for £45,000 in 1966.

He'd play only one game for the Pensioners, though, being brought to Manchester by Matt Busby as the replacement for David Gaskell, and would remain a regular for the next dozen seasons. Highspots naturally included the win against Benfica in May 1968, but Stepney had double cause for celebration: earlier in the month he'd gained his one and only full England cap in a 3-1 win against Sweden.

He played in the United side that went down and bounced back again under Tommy Docherty, two penalties in the relegation season of 1973-74 making him indisputably United's most successful goalscoring goalkeeper until Peter Schmeichel's recent challenge.

Stepney's European record is doughnut-shaped! Having played nine games in the successful European Cup campaign of 1968 and six the following season, he played eight more games divided across the 1976-77 and 1977-78 seasons as United, now back in the top flight, once more faced Continental opposition.

After losing his place to young Irishman Paddy Roche in 1978, Stepney played for Dallas Tornado in the North American Soccer League before returning to the north-west at non-League Altrincham.

Having worked on the commercial side of soccer at Rochdale, Stepney remains on the Manchester scene today, most recently as City's goalkeeping coach.

Nobby Stiles

PERSONAL FILE

Born: 18 May 1942
Birthplace: Manchester
Height: 5' 6"
Weight: 10st 10lb

LEAGUE RECORD

FROM-TO	CLUB	APPS	GOALS
1959-71	Manchester Utd	311	17
1971-73	Middlesbrough	57	2
1973-75	Preston NE	46	1
Total		414	20

MANCHESTER UNITED LEAGUE DEBUT

1 October 1960 v Bolton Wanderers

ENGLAND DEBUT

10 April 1965 v Scotland

ENGLAND HONOURS

SEASON	CAPS
1964-65	4
1965-66	16
1966-67	4
1967-68	1
1968-69	1
1969-70	2
Total	28

DID YOU KNOW?
A former fan, Nobby was delighted when United scored five against rivals City – but the opponents' single reply 'really ruined the occasion.'

The image of 'Nobby dancing' conjured up in the 1996 football song 'Three Lions' encapsulated the finest hour of Norbert Stiles, perhaps the most unlikely member of England's World Cup-winning team of 30 years earlier.

Never the prettiest of players, his abilities as a ball-winner were recognised first by Matt Busby and then Alf Ramsey, and he did a sterling job for both despite being short, balding, short-sighted and lacking his front teeth!

Though regarded as a defensive player, it was Stiles' holding role that enabled Bobby Charlton to surge forward to strike knowing his place in midfield would be filled. And when pressure was at its greatest he would be back scrapping alongside Bill Foulkes, clearing the United lines and setting up yet another attack.

Stiles was certainly not toothless on the pitch, and took few prisoners in nearly 400 games for United (in all competitions), gaining two Championship medals and playing his part in the European Cup win of 1968. He'd come through the apprentice ranks to turn pro in 1959, but it would be another six years before he earned the first of 28 full international caps. Though scoring goals was not part of his job description, one memorable derby game against Manchester City in 1961 saw him net at both ends in a 3-2 victory.

Moving on to Middlesbrough at the end of the 1970-71 season, he could not lift their fortunes due to a combination of injury and loss of form. He moved to Preston two years later to play under Bobby Charlton, and would eventually follow him into the Deepdale hot seat, yet, despite promotion to Division Two, he lost his job when they subsided four years later. Moving to West Bromwich under brother-in-law Johnny Giles, he succeeded him briefly as manager before returning to look after Old Trafford's youth team in 1989.

Hard but fair, Stiles remains a much-loved figure who's often seen on the after-dinner speaking circuit. His years with United and England provided him with much to talk about.

Gordon Strachan

PERSONAL FILE

Born: 9 February 1957
Birthplace: Edinburgh
Height: 5' 6"
Weight: 10st 6lb

LEAGUE RECORD

FROM-TO	CLUB	APPS	GOALS
1975-77	Dundee	60	13
1977-84	Aberdeen	183	55
1984-89	Manchester Utd	160	33
1989-95	Leeds Utd	197	37
1995-97	Coventry C	26	—
Total		626	138

MANCHESTER UNITED LEAGUE DEBUT

25 August 1984 v Watford

SCOTLAND DEBUT

17 May 1980 v Northern Ireland

SCOTLAND HONOURS

SEASON	CAPS
1979-80	5
1980-81	2
1981-82	7
1982-83	10
1983-84	4
1984-85	3
1985-86	6
1986-87	3
1987-88	1
1988-89	1
1989-90	1
1990-91	3
1991-92	4
Total	50

STAR QUOTE

'You can have all the skills in the world, but if you haven't got the will to win you're wasting your time.'

As mentioned earlier in this book, Manchester United have done rather well out of former Leeds players such as Gordon McQueen, Joe Jordan, Denis Irwin and Eric Cantona, but the Elland Road outfit certainly got the better of the argument over Scotland international midfielder Gordon Strachan.

Edinburgh-born Strachan began his career at Dundee but it was at Aberdeen, under one Alex Ferguson, that he came into his own. In a 300-game stay, Strachan scored 89 goals and racked up two League titles, three consecutive Scottish Cups and a European Cup Winners' Cup. Little wonder that Ron Atkinson considered him a bargain at £600,000 to replace Ray Wilkins, offloaded to Milan in May 1984.

The transfer ended an undignified tug of war for Strachan's services between United and Cologne. The German club claimed the Scot had signed for them, but the player admitted 'it has been my ambition to play on the Continent for the last two years…United came along at the last moment and you don't turn down a chance like that.' After signing a four-year post-dated contract for United, he stayed on at Pittodrie, where he'd had an on-off relationship with manager Alex Ferguson, to help Aberdeen's cause in the Scottish Cup Final against Celtic.

Strachan personified all that is good in Scottish football. Terrier-like in the tackle, his dribbling and wall-passing skills tied defenders in knots and he brought total commitment to every game he played. He quickly won FA Cup honours and became a huge favourite with the crowd until, nearly 200 games and 38 goals later, he was off to Elland Road for just £300,000, sold by his former mentor, Ferguson.

At 32, Strachan proved an inspiration at Leeds, being voted Footballer of the Year as they returned to the First Division, and helping them to the Championship in 1991-92.

Capped 50 times in all by his country, Strachan continued to play into his 40s and, in 1997, memorably led his troops from the front in the role of player-manager, as Coventry escaped relegation on the last day of the season.

Dennis Viollet

DID YOU KNOW?
Soccer clearly ran in the Viollet family's blood, since Dennis' daughter became a leading player in the UK ladies' game.

Though it should be whispered quietly, United stalwart Dennis Viollet came from a family of City supporters. What's more, his favourite club turned him down despite the promise of five England Schoolboy caps. They'd live to regret that decision as Viollet followed his time at Old Trafford with five years at Stoke City.

The Manchester born and bred inside-forward made his debut late in the 1952-53 season, while still a teenager, and the following term linked with the club's record signing Tommy Taylor to goalscoring effect. He continued to burst the net through the remainder of the decade, and his total of 32 in the 1959-60 season is still a United League record. He'd top the 20-goal mark in four of the eight complete League seasons in which he was a first-team regular, and once scored four in one match against Anderlecht as United tried European competition for the first time.

Having survived the Munich air crash, Viollet was surprisingly allowed to leave in January 1962, joining the Stoke team in which Stanley Matthews was having an indian summer. After captaining the Potters into the top flight during his time with them, he migrated across the Atlantic to play for Baltimore Bays, but a short spell as manager of Crewe after hanging up his boots was

unsuccessful. He would return to America where he remains today, coaching Jacksonville University and running soccer camps.

Dennis Viollet served United for 13 years, in which he picked up two Championship medals and an FA Cup loser's medal. His passing ability and deceptive body swerve made him an international-class player, but he won just two England caps, against Hungary in May 1960 and Luxembourg the following year. He scored in the second game, a 4-1 World Cup qualifying win.

Norman Whiteside

PERSONAL FILE

Born: 7 May 1965
Birthplace: Belfast
Height: 6' 0"
Weight: 12st 8lb

LEAGUE RECORD

FROM-TO	CLUB	APPS	GOALS
1982-89	Manchester Utd	206	47
1989-91	Everton	29	9
Total		235	56

MANCHESTER UNITED LEAGUE DEBUT

24 April 1982 v Brighton & Hove Albion

NORTHERN IRELAND DEBUT

17 June 1982 v Yugoslavia

NORTHERN IRELAND HONOURS

SEASON	CAPS
1981-82	5
1982-83	3
1983-84	7
1984-85	6
1985-86	8
1986-87	4
1987-88	3
1988-89	—
1989-90	2
Total	38

DID YOU KNOW?

Norman was particularly friendly with fellow Irishman Paul McGrath. These days, the former hellraisers run into each other at the gym!

Of all the prodigious young talents to emerge from Old Trafford since the war, the meteoric rise and fall of Norman Whiteside ranks as one of the most incredible yet, ultimately, one of the saddest.

Born in Belfast in May 1965, Whiteside was still 16 when he came on as a sub at Brighton in April 1982. After playing just once more, and scoring, that season, the strapping young forward was included in Northern Ireland's squad for the World Cup Finals in Spain. Beating Pele's record as the youngest player to grace the Finals, Whiteside appeared in all five games as his country reached the last eight.

The following season proved just as remarkable. Whiteside scored in both the 2-1 League Cup Final defeat by Liverpool and the 4-0 FA Cup Final replay win over Brighton, the youngest player to score in the Final of each event and first to score in both in the same year. Two years later, 'Big Norm' was to net the only goal, as ten-man United beat Everton in the FA Cup Final.

By 1986, Whiteside, strong and skilful, aggressive yet cultured, was prone to injury. Just as worrying was his ultra-competitive approach, which won few admirers and resulted in several suspensions. Stunned by new manager Alex Ferguson's decision to drop him, Whiteside asked for a transfer but attracted no buyers. Increasingly forced out of the picture by injury, he finally left for Everton in 1989 but played less than 30 League games before announcing his retirement at 26.

Whiteside was an early inspiration to team-mate and fellow Irishman Paul McGrath: the two shared digs, while McGrath set up a goal for him in the first youth game they played together. But while McGrath played on into his late thirties his pal was denied that chance. Whiteside now has plans to be a chiropodist, has studied podiatry at Salford University and undertakes after-dinner speaking.

In his early days, Whiteside – 67 goals in 270-odd games for United – was a mighty talent who, given better luck and perhaps better judgement, could well have moulded a career similar to that of Mark Hughes.

1979-1984

Ray Wilkins

PERSONAL FILE

Born: 14 September 1956
Birthplace: Hillingdon
Height: 5' 8"
Weight: 11st 2lb

LEAGUE RECORD

FROM-TO	CLUB	APPS	GOALS
1973-79	Chelsea	179	30
1979-84	Manchester Utd	160	7
1984-87	AC Milan	73	2
1987-89	Rangers	70	2
1989-94	QPR	154	7
1994	Crystal Palace	1	—
1994-96	QPR	21	—
1996-97	Hibernian	16	—
1997	Millwall	3	—
1997	Leyton Orient	3	—
Total		680	48

MANCHESTER UNITED LEAGUE DEBUT

18 August 1979 v Southampton

ENGLAND DEBUT

28 May 1976 v Italy

ENGLAND HONOURS

SEASON	CAPS
1975-76	1
1976-77	6
1977-78	8
1978-79	9
1979-80	11
1980-81	7
1981-82	10
1982-83	2
1983-84	8
1984-85	10
1985-86	10
1986-87	2
Total	84

DID YOU KNOW?

The cash United received from Ray paid for not one but three replacements – Alan Brazil, Jesper Olsen and Gordon Strachan.

Though Ray Wilkins is recognised as one of England's finest ever midfielders, with 84 caps and two World Cup Finals including a spell as skipper, it remains debatable whether Manchester United got the best out of him.

Nicknamed 'Butch', he was a teenage prodigy at Chelsea, where he was skipper at 18 and capped by his country at 19. He was rated the best young player in England and compared to Johnny Haynes for his remarkable perception and passing ability. It was no surprise when former Blues boss Dave Sexton took the attack-minded midfielder to Old Trafford in a then club-record £825,000 transfer in August 1979.

However, he took time to fit in at United and was often criticised for being negative, a crime never attributed to him at Stamford Bridge. When Ron Atkinson took over from the sacked Sexton in 1981 and nicknamed his captain 'the Crab', his days appeared numbered. But Ray's brilliant organisational skills in the middle of the park more than atoned for the infrequency of his forward forays and lack of goals, a job brilliantly assumed by Bryan Robson.

Following a fine season in 1983-84, Wilkins – with just one FA Cup winner's medal in the bag – departed for AC Milan for £1.5 million after 190 appearances and ten goals. He spent three superb years in Italy, remaining an England regular, and in late 1987 joined Glasgow Rangers where he won League and Cup honours.

Wilkins managed QPR in the 1990s but could never shake the playing habit and was turning out for Millwall and Orient in 1997, now into his 40s. A charming, astute man, Wilkins is much sought-after by TV companies for his dry, intelligent summaries of top matches.

Top 20 League Appearances

1	Bobby Charlton	1954-73	606
2	Bill Foulkes	1951-70	566
3	Joe Spence	1919-32	481
4	Alex Stepney	1966-78	433
5	John Silcock	1919-33	423
6	Tony Dunne	1960-72	414
7	Jack Rowley	1937-54	380
8	Arthur Albiston	1974-88	379
9	Martin Buchan	1972-83	376
10	George Best	1963-74	361
11	Allenby Chilton	1939-54	353
12	Mark Hughes	1980-86, 1988-95	345
12	Bryan Robson	1981-94	345
14	Brian McClair	1987-97	342
14	Sammy McIlroy	1971-82	342
16	Lou Macari	1972-83	329
17	Steve Coppell	1975-83	322
18	Stan Pearson	1937-53	315
19	Nobby Stiles	1959-71	311
20	Steve Bruce	1987-96	309
20	Denis Law	1962-73	309
20	Charlie Moore	1919-29	309
20	Alf Steward	1920-31	309

League Cup Record 1968-97 – The Highs and Lows

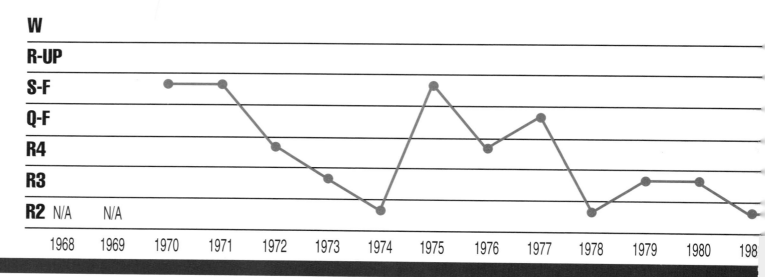

W														
R-UP														
S-F														
Q-F														
R4														
R3														
R2	N/A	N/A												
	1968	1969	1970	1971	1972	1973	1974	1975	1976	1977	1978	1979	1980	198

Top 20 League Scorers

1	Bobby Charlton	1954-73	199
2	Jack Rowley	1937-54	182
3	Denis Law	1962-73	171
4	Dennis Viollet	1952-62	159
5	Joe Spence	1919-32	158
6	George Best	1963-74	137
7	Stan Pearson	1937-53	128
8	Mark Hughes	1980-86, 1988-95	119
9	David Herd	1961-67	114
10	Tommy Taylor	1952-57	112
11	J Cassidy	1892-99	90
11	Sandy Turnbull	1906-14	90
13	George Wall	1905-14	89
14	Brian McClair	1987-97	88
15	Lou Macari	1972-83	78
16	Bryan Robson	1981-94	74
17	Enoch West	1910-14	72
18	Eric Cantona	1992-97	64
19	Tom Reid	1928-32	63
20	Frank Stapleton	1981-87	60

Above: United's squad of 1980-81 pose with manager Dave Sexton (far right, middle row). Though they finished eighth and reached the Fourth Round of the FA Cup, this was not enough to keep the well-respected Sexton in the hot seat.

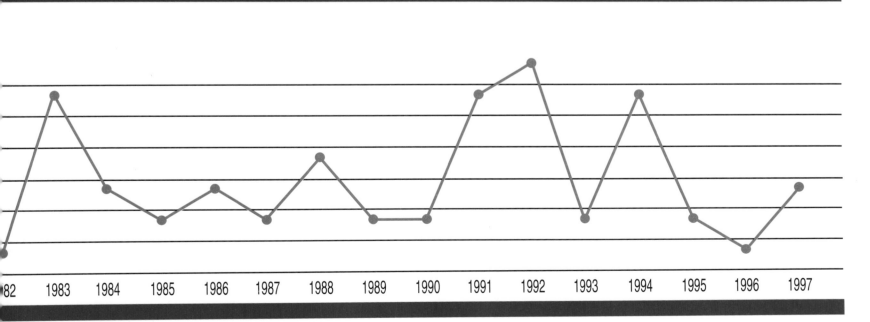

| 82 | 1983 | 1984 | 1985 | 1986 | 1987 | 1988 | 1989 | 1990 | 1991 | 1992 | 1993 | 1994 | 1995 | 1996 | 1997 |

League Record 1968-97

DIVISION ONE				Introduction of 3 points per win			
Season	**Pos**	**Pts**	**F-A**	1981-82	3rd	78	59-29
1967-68	2nd	56	89-55	1982-83	3rd	70	56-38
1968-69	11th	42	57-53	1983-84	4th	74	71-41
1969-70	8th	45	66-61	1984-85	4th	76	77-47
1970-71	8th	43	65-66	1985-86	4th	76	70-36
1971-72	8th	48	69-61	1986-87	11th	56	52-45
1972-73	18th	37	44-60	1987-88	2nd	81	71-38
1973-74	21st	32	38-48	1988-89	11th	51	45-35
				1989-90	13th	48	46-47
DIVISION TWO				1990-91	6th	59*	58-45
Season	**Pos**	**Pts**	**F-A**	1991-92	2nd	78	63-33
1974-75	1st	61	66-30	*1 point deducted for disciplinary reasons			

DIVISION ONE				FA PREMIER LEAGUE			
Season	**Pos**	**Pts**	**F-A**	**Season**	**Pos**	**Pts**	**F-A**
1975-76	3rd	56	68-42	1992-93	1st	84	67-31
1976-77	6th	47	71-62	1993-94	1st	92	80-38
1977-78	10th	42	67-63	1994-95	2nd	88	80-39
1978-79	9th	45	60-63	1995-96	1st	82	73-35
1979-80	2nd	58	65-35	1996-97	1st	75	76-44
1980-81	8th	48	51-36				

Left: Steve Bruce, now with Birmingham, stands joint 20th in United's all-time League appearances chart. As captain, he raised many trophies during his Old Trafford tenure.

FA Cup Record 1968-97 – The Highs and Lows

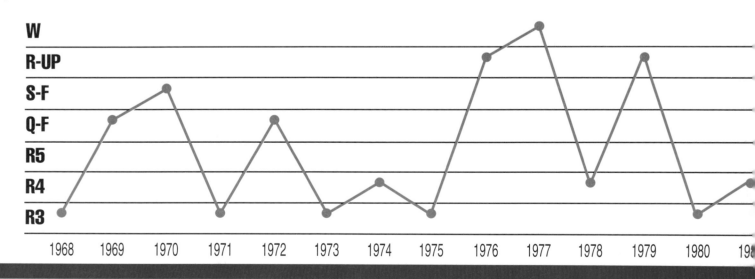

FA Cup Milestones 1968-97 *(see details of Highs & Lows below)*

Season	Opponents	Score	Season	Opponents	Score
1967-68	Tottenham H	2-2, 0-1	1982-83	Brighton &HA	2-2, 4-0
1968-69	Everton	0-1	1983-84	Bournemouth	0-2
1969-70	Leeds Utd	0-0, 0-0, 0-1	1984-85	Everton	1-0
1970-71	Middlesbrough	0-0, 1-2	1985-86	West Ham Utd	1-1, 0-2
1971-72	Stoke C	1-1, 1-2	1986-87	Coventry C	0-1
1972-73	Wolves	0-1	1987-88	Arsenal	1-2
1973-74	Ipswich T	0-1	1988-89	Nottingham Forest	0-1
1974-75	Walsall	0-0, 2-3	1989-90	Crystal Palace	3-3, 1-0
1975-76	Southampton	0-1	1990-91	Norwich C	1-2
1976-77	Liverpool	2-1	1991-92	Southampton	0-0, 2-2 (2-4 pens)
1977-78	West Brom	1-1, 2-3	1992-93	Sheffield Utd	1-2
1978-79	Arsenal	2-3	1993-94	Chelsea	4-0
1979-80	Tottenham H	1-1, 0-1	1994-95	Everton	0-1
1980-81	Nottingham Forest	0-1	1995-96	Liverpool	1-0
1981-82	Watford	0-1	1996-97	Wimbledon	1-1, 0-1

Left: United march out at Wembley. Their one League Cup victory to date was in 1992 against Nottingham Forest, having been beaten Finalists the year before.

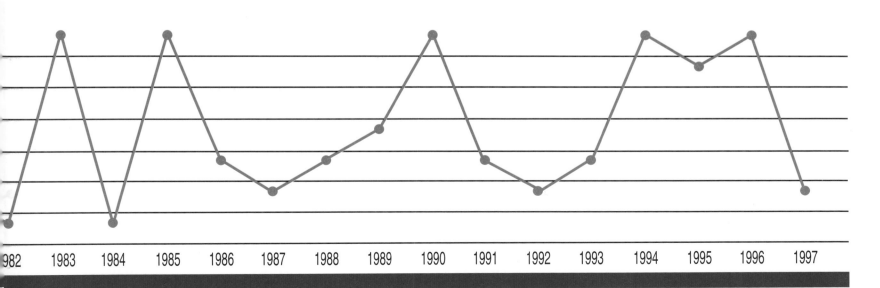

982   1983   1984   1985   1986   1987   1988   1989   1990   1991   1992   1993   1994   1995   1996   1997

Above: High-flying Eire international striker Frank Stapleton scored 60 League goals after joining United from Arsenal in 1981.

Honours

1896-97	Division Two Runners-up
1905-06	Division Two Runners-up
1907-08	Division One Champions
1908-09	FA Cup Winners
1910-11	Division One Champions
1924-25	Division Two Runners-up
1935-36	Division Two Champions
1937-38	Division Two Runners-up
1946-47	Division One Runners-up
1947-48	Division One Runners-up and FA Cup Winners
1948-49	Division One Runners-up
1950-51	Division One Runners-up
1951-52	Division One Champions
1955-56	Division One Champions
1956-57	Division One Champions and FA Cup Runners-up
1957-58	FA Cup Runners-up
1958-59	Division One Runners-up
1962-63	FA Cup Winners
1963-64	Division One Runners-up
1964-65	Division One Champions
1966-67	Division One Champions
1967-68	Division One Runners-up, European Cup Winners and World Club Championship Runners-up
1974-75	Division Two Champions
1975-76	FA Cup Runners-up
1976-77	FA Cup Winners
1978-79	FA Cup Runners-up
1979-80	Division One Runners-up
1982-83	FA Cup Winners and League Cup Runners-up
1984-85	FA Cup Winners
1987-88	Division One Runners-up
1989-90	FA Cup Winners
1990-91	League Cup Runners-up, European Cup Winners' Cup Winners and Super Cup Winners
1991-92	Division One Runners-up and League Cup Winners
1992-93	Premier League Champions
1993-94	Premier League Champions, FA Cup Winners and League Cup Runners-up
1994-95	Premier League Runners-up and FA Cup Runners-up
1995-96	Premier League Champions and FA Cup Winners
1996-97	Premier League Champions